*American Arms and a
Changing Europe*

INSTITUTE OF WAR AND PEACE STUDIES
of the School of International Affairs of
Columbia University

American Arms and a Changing Europe: Dilemmas of Deterrence and Disarmament is one of a series of studies sponsored by the Institute of War and Peace Studies of Columbia University. Among those Institute studies also dealing with war, peace, and national security are *Defense and Diplomacy* by Alfred Vagts; *Man, the State and War* by Kenneth N. Waltz; *The Common Defense* by Samuel P. Huntington; *Changing Patterns of Military Politics* edited by Samuel P. Huntington; *Strategy, Politics and Defense Budgets* by Warner R. Schilling, Paul Y. Hammond, and Glenn H. Snyder; *Stockpiling Strategic Materials* by Glenn H. Snyder; *The Politics of Military Unification* by Demetrios Caraley; *NATO and the Range of American Choice* by William T. R. Fox and Annette Baker Fox; *The Politics of Weapons Innovation: The Thor-Jupiter Controversy* by Michael H. Armacost; *The Politics of Policy Making in Defense and Foreign Affairs* by Roger Hilsman; *Inspection for Disarmament* edited by Seymour Melman; *To Move a Nation* by Roger Hilsman, jointly sponsored with the Washington Center of Foreign Policy Research, Johns Hopkins University; *Planning, Prediction and Policy-making in Foreign Affairs* by Robert L. Rothstein; *The Origins of Peace* by Robert F. Randle; and *European Security and the Atlantic System* edited by William T. R. Fox and Warner R. Schilling. Institute studies now in press include *German Nuclear Weapons Policy* by Catherine M. Kelleher; *Technology, the Future, and American Policy* by Victor Basiuk; and *The Cold War Begins: Soviet-American Conflict over Eastern Europe* by Lynn Etheridge Davis.

american arms
and a
changing europe
dilemmas of deterrence and disarmament

Warner R. Schilling / William T. R. Fox /
Catherine M. Kelleher / Donald J. Puchala

COLUMBIA UNIVERSITY PRESS

New York and London / 1973

Library of Congress Cataloging in Publication Data
Main entry under title:

American arms and a changing Europe. · ·   /by Warner A.
   "Revised version of a report written by members of   Schilling [and
the Institute of War and Peace Studies, Columbia   others]
University, under contract with the United States Arms
Control and Disarmament Agency and submitted . . . in
November 1971."
   Includes bibliographical references.
   1. Europe—Defenses.   2. United States—Military
policy.   3. Deterrence (Strategy)   4. Disarmament.
I. Schilling, Warner Roller, 1925–
UA646.A64   355.03'3073   73-4303
ISBN 0-231-03704-x
ISBN 0-231-03705-8 (pbk)

pReface

THIS BOOK ANALYZES how European security arrangements may change in the decade ahead and the arms control problems and opportunities that may come with these changes. The book is a somewhat revised version of a report written by members of the Institute of War and Peace Studies, Columbia University, under contract with the United States Arms Control and Disarmament Agency and submitted to that agency in November 1971. The study made no use of classified material, and the judgments expressed in this book are those of the authors and do not necessarily reflect the views of ACDA or any other agency or department of the United States government.

The analysis in this book borrows freely from the contents of the supporting papers commissioned in accordance with the overall research design of the project. The first part of this book's Chapter Three, for example, is closely paraphrased from the supporting paper written by Klaus Knorr. Most of these supporting papers have been published in a companion volume entitled *European Security and the Atlantic System,* and readers interested in an extended discussion of many of the points presented in this book can find it in the companion volume.

Responsibility for the seven chapters in this book is not easily fixed. The first draft of Chapter Three was written by Catherine M. Kelleher; the first draft of Chapter Five by Donald J. Puchala; the first drafts of Chapters Four and Six by William T. R. Fox; and the first drafts of Chapters One, Two, and Seven by Warner R. Schilling. Subsequent changes were made in all of these chapters by the original authors and by the last two writers, especially by Warner Schilling, who served as the Project Director.

In a larger sense the responsibilities of authorship are joint. The general approach of this volume and the main ideas expressed in it are the result of the many meetings which the authors held with the other Columbia and New York participants in this project to discuss the supporting papers. A full list of those who worked on the project can be found in the preface to *European Security and the Atlantic System*. The authors also want to acknowledge the great help they received from the participants in a conference at Lake Mohonk, New Paltz, N.Y., in the fall of 1969, at which a preliminary draft of this volume was exposed to chapter-by-chapter criticism. The participants at this conference, which was sponsored by the Institute of War and Peace Studies as part of the project, are listed in the Institute's report to ACDA and are not, of course, responsible for the contents of this volume.

A note of appreciation is in order to two former employees of ACDA, John Lippman and Harland Moulton, who served as liaison officers for the project and provided it with administrative support and intellectual assistance. It is also a pleasure to acknowledge the research assistance of Joan Edelman Spero, Marilyn Wellons, Irmtraud Toelle Shattuck, Patrick Murphy, Roger Cohen, and John Rounsaville.

The authors well know how large a debt they owe to Jane P. M. Schilling, whose skillful editing contributed so much to the sense and structure of this volume; to Anna Hohri, the Administrative Assistant for the Institute, who backstopped the project and its director on a variety of issues and occasions with the kind of advice and assistance that is no less remarkable for being customary; to Myra B. Ramos, who served as the administrative assistant for the project until February 1970 and who provided the kind of organizational, intellectual, and personal support that could be believed only by those who experienced it; and to Linda Wangsness Threlkeld, who undertook with intelligence, skill, and good humor the administrative and typing burdens connected with the preparation of this volume. Mrs. Threlkeld also faced the problem of attending to the volume's completion during the intermittent poor health of the Project Director, and for her cheerful moral support during this difficult time a very special note of thanks is due.

William T. R. Fox
Catherine M. Kelleher
Donald J. Puchala
Warner R. Schilling

contents

*American Arms and a
Changing Europe*

intRoduction

AMERICAN FOREIGN POLICY has been directed toward two major strategic goals since the end of World War II: preservation of the balance of power in Europe, and prevention of a Soviet-American nuclear war. The pursuit of these two goals has been complicated, however, by the inability of the United States and its allies to provide for the security of the Western Europeans except through an American commitment to use strategic nuclear weapons in their defense. As a result, the United States has confronted a strategic dilemma: policies designed to maintain the security of Western Europe have frequently seemed to strain the stability of the Soviet-American strategic balance, and policies designed to improve the stability of the Soviet-American strategic balance have seemed to threaten the security of Western Europe.

This conflict has, in turn, complicated the effort of the United States to moderate through arms control the risks and costs involved in the pursuit of these goals. In the confrontation in Europe between the NATO powers and the Warsaw Treaty Organization (WTO) powers and that between the United States and the Soviet Union in the nuclear balance of terror, the parties involved have a common interest in finding ways in which they can reduce the risk of the nuclear war which no one wants, the cost of the arms believed necessary to prevent that war, and the extent and scope of destruction should war nonetheless in some manner start.

The problems and choices that the United States will meet during the decade ahead in the pursuit of these three goals—

European security, strategic security, and arms control—constitute the subject of this book. The major focus of the analysis is on the forms that future European security arrangements may take and how American choices in arms and arms control policy can affect the form of those arrangements. But since arms and arms control policies cannot be developed (or analyzed) for either European or strategic security in isolation one from another, considerable attention is also given to the changes that may occur in the strategic balance and how they may affect both the future course of European security arrangements and the opportunities for strategic arms control.

The chapters that follow are addressed to several major questions: what has been the past relationship between American policies designed to maintain the European balance of power and those designed to maintain the Soviet-American balance of terror, and how has American policy tried to ease the potential incompatibility between them? (Chapter One); what are the changes that may occur in the strategic balance, and how may these changes affect future European security arrangements? (Chapter Two); what are the major economic and political trends and developments that may materialize in Europe, the United States, and the Soviet Union over the next decade, and how may they affect future European security arrangements? (Chapter Three); toward what other forms might present European security arrangements change? (Chapter Four); how might the military, economic, and political trends and developments previously described combine to lead to one or another of these possible forms? (Chapter Five); what is the most immediately likely shape of future European security arrangements, and what problems and opportunities does this semi-determined future present for American policy? (Chapter Six); what arms control perspectives, processes, and choices can most effectively implement the American interest in both European and strategic security and ease the strain among policies designed to serve those objectives? (Chapter Seven).

The answers to these questions have been sought through the application of a variety of methods ranging from historical review and the exercise of what can be generously described as disciplined imagination to the construction of theoretical models and an application of systems analysis. Information for the study was collected primarily from a reading of relevant monographs, articles, and government publications, and supplemented by discussions with government officials and other scholars, both in the United States and abroad. The analysis in this book is particularly indebted for both information and ideas to the contents of the companion volume described in the preface.

The analytical purpose of the book is not to predict *the* future but to delimit the range of possible futures and within that range to identify the major choices the United States will confront in the decade ahead in its effort to maintain both the security of Western Europe and the stability of the Soviet-American strategic balance. The policy purpose of the book is to prescribe some arms and arms control policies that can reduce the political and military costs and risks entailed in the pursuit of these objectives.

To pursue multiple objectives simultaneously often involves hard choices. European security, strategic security, and arms control are not, of course, ends in themselves; all are desirable only insofar as they contribute to American security. But while in theory there may be no basic incompatibility among objectives designed to serve a common end, in practice the means to achieve such objectives repeatedly turn out to be difficult to reconcile. Indeed, as later chapters demonstrate, the common pursuit of arms control, European security, and strategic security bristles with dilemmas.

There is the strategic dilemma previously noted. In particular, how can the United States limit nuclear arms except on the basis of parity, and how can it guarantee the security of Western Europe except on a basis of nuclear superiority?

There is the central political dilemma. How can the United States achieve a détente with the Soviet Union except by acquiescing in a divided Europe, but how can Western Europe achieve a détente with Eastern Europe except by breaking down that division?

There is the escalation-deterrence dilemma. In the event of a conflict in Europe, it would be desirable to have some missing rungs in the ladder of escalation to thermonuclear exchange, but how can they be taken out without weakening the deterrent to acts so consequential that the United States would use whatever force proved necessary to counter them?

There is the uncertainty dilemma. To make every American capability and intention clear is to insure that the Soviet Union will not miscalculate, but it will also weaken at the margins the deterrent effectiveness of American military power and may indeed actually invite aggression just beyond the margin.

There is the consultation dilemma. Arrangements that oblige the United States to consult with its allies before taking actions of common consequence may serve to protect the interests of its allies and their desire for equality, but an agreement to consult before taking action to fulfill a commitment may also raise questions about the absoluteness of that commitment.

There is the damage-limitation dilemma. It is good to be in a position to save American lives and property if there should be a thermonuclear exchange and, by having acted effectively to limit the human and material costs, to add to the credibility of America's promise to hold a nuclear umbrella over its European allies; but it is bad to seek to destabilize the strategic balance if an imbalance drives the opponent into preventive countersteps that endanger both the United States and its allies.

Finally, there is the Western European self-defense dilemma. If Americans underestimate Western Europe's power to defend itself, the United States may greatly narrow the range of possible nuclear arms limitations; but if Americans overestimate Western Europe's power to protect itself, the United States may endanger the peace in an area which has already involved the United States in two world wars.

It is not given of course that every American policy for the security of Western Europe, for the stability of the strategic balance, or for arms control is on a collision course with every other. Policies may be wholly compatible; they may even be reinforcing. Only patient analysis can reveal which of the dilemmas sketched above are more apparent than real, which can be successfully avoided, which can be eased, and which pose inescapable and painful choices. It is to this task, however inadequate the performance, that this book is dedicated.

/ Chapter One

the stRateGic dilemma

I

      SINCE THE END OF WORLD WAR II, the United States has encountered a continuing dilemma in its effort to reconcile its policies for the preservation of the European balance of power with its policies for the prevention of a Soviet-American nuclear war. Part of the problem has been that although the policies designed for the pursuit of these goals have partly overlapped in content, the two security problems to which they are addressed developed sequentially in time and are different in character and divergent in their import for American interests in Europe. But the root of the dilemma has been the inability of the United States to find a way to defend Western Europe except through a commitment to resort, if necessary, to the use of strategic nuclear weapons, for this commitment has seemed to require the United States to maintain, in effect, not a balance but an imbalance of terror. The result, as stated in the Introduction, has been that policies designed to maintain the security of Western Europe have frequently strained the stability of the Soviet-American strategic balance, and policies designed to improve the stability of the Soviet-American strategic balance have seemed to threaten the security of Western Europe.

    The purpose of this chapter is to outline the background for the American commitment to the European balance of power, the manner in which policies on behalf of that commitment have affected the Soviet-American strategic balance, and the main features of previous efforts by the United States to ease the conflict between its balance-of-power policies and its balance-of-terror policies. This first chapter is intended, then, to provide a brief review of the past and to introduce a problem with which both later chapters and future American policy will be concerned.

II

The American commitment to defend Western Europe, although made after the development of nuclear weapons, was essentially prenuclear in its strategic rationale. In the immediate postwar years, the once mighty nations of Western Europe seemed in no condition to balance the military power of the Soviet Union, even in the face of the severe material and personnel losses which that nation itself had suffered. The United States met this situation both through policies designed to substitute American power for European power (first by the continued presence of American military forces in Europe, and later with the commitments of the Truman Doctrine and the North Atlantic Treaty) and through policies designed to restore to the Western European nations themselves the capacity to balance the Russians (the Marshall Plan and the Mutual Defense Assistance Program).

It is a fair presumption that these actions would have been taken even if the close of World War II had not demonstrated the feasibility of nuclear weapons, and they appear to have been little influenced by the fact that this demonstration had taken place. The American commitment to defend the nations of Western Europe reflected lessons that statesmen believed they had learned from World War I and World War II rather than an anticipation of the needs for American security in the nuclear age to come. There seemed little point in permitting the Russians to achieve at their will what had just been so painfully wrested from the hands of the Germans: an empire embracing all the people, skills, and resources of the Old World. In addition to the desire not to see the results of World War II undone, American policy was also moved by the expectation that by committing itself in advance to the preservation of what was left of the European balance of power, the United States would be able to escape having to fight to maintain it. The Russians would be given an "advantage" that neither the Kaiser's nor Hitler's Germany had enjoyed: knowing that they would have to fight the Americans, the Russians would be deterred from starting a war in Europe.

The development by the Soviet Union of a strategic nuclear capability brought, however, a qualitative change in the significance of the European balance of power for American military security. The character of the weapons technology of World Wars I and II was such that no single European nation could hope to mount a successful attack on the American continent. Only if all the people, skills, and resources of the Great Powers in Europe were combined, by alliance or conquest, could an overseas enemy hope to match the military potential of the United States. The result, if not in all instances the intent, of American intervention in World Wars I and II had been to prevent this contingency.

In contrast to the weapons technology of World Wars I and II, nuclear weapons systems are so cheap in terms of the destruction they can achieve that the Soviet Union can mobilize from inside its own frontiers sufficient military power to devastate the United States. If the Soviet Union were to secure command over the people, skills, and resources of Western Europe, it would greatly reduce the cost the Soviets would incur in maintaining nuclear forces sufficient to destroy the United States, but it would not qualitatively affect their ability to maintain such forces.

Today the military security of the United States pivots on the stability of the Soviet-American balance of terror, not on the presence or absence of a balance of power in Europe. This is not to suggest that the postwar commitment to defend Western Europe was either imprudent or unwise. Given their fears regarding Soviet expansion and their ideological as well as military stake in the area, Americans would have been foolish not to have made that commitment. But it is necessary to take note of the obvious: the contribution of the European balance of power to American military security has decreased, while the potential costs of maintaining it have greatly increased. The commitment to defend Western Europe cannot prevent a nuclear attack on the United States, but a war undertaken in order to meet that commitment could well result in such an attack.

III

For two decades the forces and doctrine considered appropriate to meet America's two major strategic objectives have been the subject of debate and controversy. During these years, the procession of divergent "official" policies and postures has been such as to unsettle and confuse even the stoutest of American allies (and perhaps enemies, as well). The frequency with which Americans have changed their minds about the appropriate forces and strategy required for the defense of Western Europe or those for the maintenance of the Soviet-American balance of terror can be charged in part to the manner in which new developments in military technology keep changing the face of these two problems. But a full explanation must take account of the continued bafflement of American policy-makers as they have endeavored to devise a political-military policy for Western Europe that fits the strategic needs of the Soviet-American balance of terror.

The main difficulty has been the inability of the United States and its European allies to provide a defense for Western Europe that does not depend ultimately on an American commitment to respond to a Soviet attack with the use of strategic nuclear weapons, even if the Soviet Union has not itself first used nuclear weapons. Although this commitment has been associated, at least in time, with twenty years of peace, the appropriateness of the commitment has come under increasing criticism, with regard to both its utility for the defense of Western Europe and its consequence for the Soviet-American strategic balance.

One line of criticism takes as its point of departure the growth of Soviet nuclear forces and the argument that if the United States started a nuclear war, the Soviet Union would strike back in sufficient force to destroy American society. Accordingly, Americans have doubted the desirability of pinning the defense of Western

Europe on such a commitment; Western Europeans have worried about the willingness of Americans to deliver on that commitment; and both have wondered about the credibility of the commitment in Soviet minds and thus about its effectiveness as a deterrent.

A second line of criticism takes as its point of departure the growth of American nuclear forces and the argument that because of the NATO commitment the United States has been intent on maintaining not a balance but an imbalance of terror. In order to insure that the Russians are deterred from starting a nuclear war but the Americans, in extremis, are not, the United States has been obliged to develop offensive strategic doctrines (massive retaliation, preemptive strike capability) and to embrace appropriate force goals (strategic superiority, counterforce and damage-limiting ability). The result has been to exacerbate Soviet-American relations (by lending substance to Soviet fears of American aggression), to stimulate an unending arms race (by seeming to threaten the Soviet goal of preventing an American nuclear attack), and to lead the Soviet Union to take actions that on at least one occasion (the emplacement of missiles in Cuba) directly threatened the goal of Soviet-American peace.

The two lines of criticism are joined in the argument that American policy has incurred the worst of both worlds. The United States has been able to maintain superiority over the Soviet Union in bombers, warheads, and (until recently) missiles, but it has not been able to maintain sufficient superiority to deprive the Soviet Union of a second-strike capability that could kill 25 to 50 percent of the American population. As a result, American policy has strained Soviet-American relations and fueled the arms race without significantly alleviating reservations about either the desirability or the credibility of the American commitment to start a nuclear war in defense of Western Europe.

It is not the point of this chapter to argue the merits of American policy one way or the other. The purpose here is only to note the strain that the American strategy for defending Western Europe has placed on its other major strategic goal, the prevention of a Soviet nuclear attack on the United States. The effort to maintain an imbalance of terror is not necessarily inconsistent with the goal of deterrence, but it does complicate its pursuit. By stimulating both Soviet fears and the arms race, American policy has made deterrence more expensive and potentially more precarious. In addition, by defining American strategic doctrine in terms that, taken literally, would appear to preclude the Soviet objective of deterring an American nuclear attack, American policy has rendered infeasible in advance any major effort to improve the stability of the Soviet-American balance of terror through an arms control agreement.

It is possible, of course, that the United States might have developed the same strategic doctrine in the absence of the commitment to defend Western Europe. There is a military case for the United States' maintaining a war-fighting as well as a war-deterring capability, even if its only concern were the defense of the American continent, and if the North Atlantic Treaty were to be dissolved, there would certainly be government officials who would continue to argue the need for a counterforce and damage-limiting capability superior to that of the Soviet Union. But in the real world the NATO commitment exists. Without access to the classified documents that have attended the debate over the development of American strategy, an outside observer cannot reach a conclusive judgment on the influence of the NATO commitment in determining the content of that strategy. One can only note the plausibility of the proposition that the NATO commitment has provided a persuasive rationale for a war-threatening (and hence a superior war-fighting) capability.

It is equally difficult, without access to the classified documents of the Politburo, for an outside observer to reach a conclusive judgment on how American strategy and forces have affected Soviet policy. It could be that Soviet leaders have read accurately the essentially defensive character of earlier doctrines (such as massive retaliation) as well as more recent statements arguing the need for an American preemptive capability, and recognizing that the choice of war or peace rests in their hands, have not seen their own security as seriously compromised either by American strategies or by the forces designed to serve those strategies.

But to presume that Soviet leaders see Americans as they really are is to endow that leadership with a greater capability for for-eign-policy analysis than has been demonstrated by any other twentieth-century statesmen and to deny that their perceptions of American purposes and programs are colored by the concepts and propositions of Marxism-Leninism. Surely the more plausible prop-osition is that the Soviet leadership has viewed the American dis-cussion and development of war-threatening and war-fighting forces and strategies as reflecting an American ambition to alter *their* status quo, as well as to protect its own, and that the result-ing fears and insecurities have influenced the size and doctrine of their own military forces, both those for strategic nuclear war and those deployed against Western Europe.

IV

American policy has not been inattentive to the strain between the nation's balance-of-power and balance-of-terror strategies, and the conflict between the two strategies has varied over time.

In the early years of the Truman administration, this conflict was at a minimum. It required, in a way, no great effort for the Truman administration to decide that the defense of Western Europe was worth the costs of World War III, for throughout most of those years World War III looked very much like World War II, and the nation had just demonstrated its conviction that the preservation of the European balance of power was worth World War II. Throughout Truman's presidency, the American nuclear stockpile was small, and the Soviets' initially nonexistent. Military planning could and did see World War III as essentially determined by the outcome of a land battle on the European continent, with nuclear weapons expected to provide for effective but not decisive strategic bombardment.

Neither the Americans nor the Europeans proved willing to provide the large ground forces that the Truman administration had advocated for the defense of Western Europe, especially after the advent of the Korean War, and it was during the Eisenhower administration that the strain between the United States' interest in avoiding nuclear war with the Soviet Union and its interest in defending Western Europe became especially evident. In effect, the Eisenhower administration decided that the defense of Western Europe was not worth the costs of World War II, but it was worth risking the costs of World War III. By this time, the growth of both Soviet and American nuclear power had made the prospective shape of World War III quite different from that of World War II. Nonetheless, under the leadership of the Eisenhower administration the NATO powers committed themselves to use nuclear weapons in their defense, whether they were used in the Soviet attack or not. In addition to pinning the defense of Western Europe to the American threat of massive nuclear retaliation, the Eisenhower administration also initiated the development of battlefield nuclear weapons as a means of counterbalancing the superior ground forces of the Soviet Army. This proved a short-run expedient, for by the end of the Eisenhower administration it was believed that the Soviets' own development of battlefield nuclear weapons had once again given the Soviet Army the capability of overrunning the ground defenses of Western Europe. In consequence, the defense of Western Europe at the end of the Eisenhower administration rested, in the final analysis, where it had begun: on the American threat to initiate a strategic nuclear war.

The most determined effort to come to grips with this problem was made during the Kennedy administration. Once again, American strategy was recast, this time in the form that the defense of Western Europe was worth the costs of World War II, but the risks of incurring the costs of World War III should be minimized. In pursuit of this conception, the Kennedy administration developed a threefold approach. First, a determined effort was made to increase the conventional-weapons forces of the NATO powers to the point where they could meet those of the Soviet Union and its allies on equal terms. It was argued that this would not be too difficult, for the NATO powers clearly had the superior resources (whether measured in people, steel, electric power, or gross national product). In addition, it was pointed out that the strength of the Red Army had been exaggerated in previous NATO estimates. Second, an effort was made to downgrade NATO's reliance on tactical nuclear weapons. Although the number of these weapons assigned to NATO was greatly increased during the Kennedy and Johnson administrations, Americans argued relentlessly that they should not be used at the start of any war. Finally, an effort was made to redesign the shape of World War III. In 1962 the Soviet Union (and America's NATO allies) were informed that if the United States should initiate the use of nuclear weapons against the Soviet Union, it would do so initially only against military targets and it would avoid the use of nuclear weapons against cities if the Soviet Union would practice a similar restraint.

These three elements of American policy were clearly designed to reduce the degree of conflict between America's two major security objectives. All three failed. The NATO allies proved unwilling to develop the conventional-weapons forces advocated by the United States. Their interests lay in preventing World War III, not in fighting it, and they were quite content to see this prevention rest on the American commitment to use nuclear weapons in their defense, especially since they assigned an increasingly lower probability to the prospect of any large-scale Soviet attack on NATO.

The Soviet Union on its part was equally unresponsive to the American suggestion that the use of nuclear weapons be restricted to counterforce targets. On a declaratory level at least, the Soviets were insistent that in the event of a nuclear attack, they would respond with an all-out assault on both American cities and military targets. This was an understandable response, since at that time the American superiority in nuclear forces was such that the Soviets could anticipate, after an extensive counterforce exchange, that they would have exhausted most or all of their forces, while the Americans would still have sufficient forces remaining to confront them with the choice of either surrendering or seeing their cities destroyed without the ability to retaliate in kind.

American relations with Britain and France during this period were further strained by the fact that Britain and France continued to develop their own strategic nuclear forces. The Americans roundly condemned this effort both for being of little political and military value (on the grounds that the European forces were and would remain too small and too vulnerable to be of consequence) and for being of positive political and military harm. These forces were seen as endangering the European balance of power (by detracting from the effort Britain and France might otherwise put into conventional weapons), as jeopardizing the Soviet-American balance of terror (by not readily lending themselves to the city-avoidance strategy and possibly endangering it through too early a use against Soviet cities), and as damaging the prospects for East-West détente (by possibly leading the West Germans to want nuclear weapons of their own, which would alarm everyone in sight).

The final effort of the Kennedy administration to ease the relationship between its plans for the defense of Western Europe and its desire to maintain the Soviet-American strategic peace took the form of the Multilateral Force. The MLF, of course, represented different things to different Americans. For some, it was simply a device for preempting the German desire for nuclear weapons, and for others it was a means of disarming the British and French nuclear forces.

But in addition, the MLF reflected two divergent "grand designs" for finally resolving the twin problems of American continental security and European defense. There were those who saw in the MLF the seedbed for developing a European union. For these people the MLF was an arrangement from which the United States might in time remove itself, in expectation that the problem of insuring effective command and control over their own nuclear weapons would lead the Europeans to form a polity that would provide for its own defense. For others, there was no expectation of an American withdrawal; the MLF was to serve as the seedbed for a more integrated Atlantic community, which would in time develop such indivisible security arrangements as to blur the difference between European and American defense.

Like the grand designs that moved its proponents, the MLF appealed mainly to Americans, and the only notable contribution of the Johnson administration to the problems under review here was quietly to bury the MLF, in the recognition that there was no point in alarming the Russians and irritating the British and French for an arrangement the Germans did not want.

The challenge of devising a strategic concept that will relate the American interest in avoiding nuclear war and its commitment to the defense of Western Europe now taxes the imagination and talents of the Nixon administration. But President Nixon's administration, no less than those of his four predecessors, does not have the luxury of addressing itself to a static problem. In addition to the problems inherited from those predecessors, the Nixon administration must grapple with the consequences of new developments in military technology and strategy that will affect not only the shape of old, familiar problems and issues but introduce new ones as well, and it is with these developments that the next chapter is concerned.

/ Chapter Two

the changing
strategic environment

THIS CHAPTER is concerned with the effects of a selected number of current and prospective developments in strategic weapons technology. The chapter endeavors to anticipate the
consequences these military developments may have for the Soviet-American strategic balance and the manner in which these
consequences may, in turn, affect present European security arrangements.

Three caveats are appropriate at the start of the discussion. The
first is that security policies and security arrangements are the
product of the political goals and expectations of nations, as well
as of their military capabilities. As a result, the effect of military
developments on security policies may be difficult to predict without reference to accompanying (but possibly quite independent)
political developments. The decisions in 1950 to rearm the Germans and to form the North Atlantic Treaty Organization, for example, owed more to the effect of the Korean War in increasing
American and European fears of a Soviet attack on Europe than
they did to the advent of the Soviet A-bomb. Similarly, the French

decision to withdraw from NATO in 1966, while reflecting differences with the United States over the growth of Soviet nuclear power and doubts about the reliability of the American commitment in the face of that power, was also moved by the French assumption that the Sino-Soviet conflict had reduced the Soviet threat to Europe and by the French ambition to become the leader in a *Europe des Patries*.

It is possible, if basic political goals and expectations remain constant, for the central characteristics of security arrangements to remain unaltered by even a large number of major changes in military technology. Since 1949, for example, there have been a variety of major military innovations: jet airplanes, thermonuclear weapons, tactical nuclear weapons, land- and sea-based IRBMs, ICBMs, and reconnaissance satellites. Yet throughout this period the central features of the structure of European security have remained unchanged. Europe has remained divided between the superpowers; each superpower has remained committed to the defense of its half; and each superpower has continued to dominate the security policies and postures of its sphere.

This is not to state that there have been no significant modifications in the features of this security arrangement or that the changes in military technology listed above have not contributed to these modifications. In the case of the United States and Western Europe, as noted in the preceding chapter, the security policies proposed by the United States to meet these military developments have encountered mounting opposition from its allies. As the United States has become increasingly vulnerable to Soviet nuclear power, many Western Europeans have questioned the reliability of the American commitment to go to war in their defense. Finally, and somewhat paradoxically, the destructive character of nuclear war has also led Western Europeans to believe that there is little danger of a Soviet military attack, and the reduced fear of war has prompted some European statesmen to develop policies designed to bridge the division of Europe.

The character of military technology is, then, a major but not always critical variable in influencing the content of security policies or the structure of security arrangements. The extent of the influence that changes in military technology can exercise on security policies depends on their consequence for the effectiveness of those policies. Changes in military technology, and more particularly the resulting changes in the strategic doctrines that guide the acquisition, deployment, and potential use of the weapons involved, can alter judgments about both the prospects for war and the course that war might take if it came. And by affecting judgments on these issues, which are central to the effectiveness of security policies, changes in military technology can potentially influence judgments about the continued desirability or utility of those policies.

The second caveat that must attend this discussion relates to the difficulty of seeing very far into the technological future. It is difficult to think of any ten-year period since the end of World War II that has been without at least one major weapons innovation that had not been anticipated, at least in the public literature, at the start of that period. Since both the rate of technological innovation and the growth of new scientific knowledge are still increasing, it is plausible that the late 1970s will see at least one major new weapons development, not currently anticipated, that will threaten to alter the strategic environment.

The discussion in this chapter focuses on four military developments immediately at hand: more reliable and accurate MIRV missiles; improved ABM systems; more sophisticated ground- and space-based intelligence systems; and more effective and extensive command and control systems.

These weapons developments—MIRVs, ABMs, and the improved intelligence and command systems that will be associated with them—are not the result of new technical developments. They will come from applying and improving existing innovations in such assorted fields as rocket propulsion and guidance, radars, cameras, and computers. But the military and foreign-policy consequences from this immediately forthcoming technology seem great enough, in terms of both their direct influence on the Soviet-American nuclear balance and their secondary influence on American policies for defending Western Europe, to justify foregoing an analysis of the potential effects of more distant and uncertain technical developments. The end of the decade will certainly see some new developments, but whatever their effect, it will be on a world already significantly altered by the MIRV-ABM technology.[1]

The third caveat appropriate to note at the start of this chapter's analysis is the difficulty of predicting what agreements will be reached at the Strategic Arms Limitation Talks and hence the effect of SALT on the future character and development of the Soviet-American strategic balance.

The stability of both the Soviet-American balance of terror and present European security arrangements would be greatly enhanced (as subsequent analysis will show) if there were an effective agreement to ban the deployment of MIRVs. But there seems little prospect for this. Whether the MIRV technology and all that will follow in its wake might have been halted in earlier years by means of a MIRV test-ban agreement must remain a subject of speculation, since the governments of neither the Soviet Union nor the United States showed any real interest in exploring this possibility during the time when the American MIRV program was still under development.

Given the American development and assuming that the Soviet Union will not agree to on-site inspection, the deployment of MIRV can now be prevented only through some form of asymmetrical arms control agreement: the Americans alone permit on-site inspection and rely on their ability to detect evasion of a flight test-ban agreement to stop Soviet development; or the Soviets rely on the American press to detect an American evasion of a nondeployment agreement, and the Americans rely on a flight test ban to prevent Soviet development. Neither agreement seems likely, for there are political and military risks for both governments in either possibility, and a decision to incur those risks would require the two governments to share a concern for the consequences of MIRV

[1] For some interesting efforts to forecast new weapons technology, see Nigel Calder (ed.), *Unless Peace Comes* (New York: Viking Press, 1968); B. T. Feld, T. Greenwood, G. W. Rathjens, and S. Weinberg (eds.), *Impact of New Technologies on the Arms Race* (Cambridge: MIT Press, 1971); and the testimony of Herman Kahn and Harold A. Linstone in House of Representatives Committee on Foreign Affairs, Subcommittee on National Security Policy and Scientific Developments, *Hearings, Strategy and Science: Toward a National Security Policy for the 1970's*, 91st Cong., 1st Sess. (1969) [hereafter cited as HCFA, *Science and Strategy*].

that they clearly have not demonstrated to date. Moreover, the opportunity for even these agreements will disappear once the Soviet Union begins to flight-test its own MIRV systems.

This chapter therefore assumes that both superpowers will deploy MIRV in the 1970s and considers only three possible outcomes from SALT: (1) no agreement at all; (2) an agreement on the American proposal to ban ABMs (or limit them to a few hundred for the defense of national capitals or ICBM fields) and to place a ceiling on the total number of delivery vehicles that each power could maintain (bombers, fixed-site ICBMs, SLBMs), with each power free to decide on its own mix, provided that the number of large ICBMs would not exceed something on the order of the present Soviet SS-9 deployment; and (3) an agreement on the Soviet proposal to ban or limit only ABMs.[2]

The objective criterion advanced for a limit on the level of offensive arms—the total number of delivery vehicles—will not readily lend itself to a meaningful and mutually acceptable agreement. The number of delivery vehicles takes no account of differences in the number, size, and accuracy of warheads. On the other hand, an agreement negotiated on the basis of the number of warheads would take no account of differences in the number and vulnerability of delivery vehicles, and the number of each side's warheads would, in any event, be difficult to verify independently.

There is the additional issue—raised by the Soviet Union—of whether the tactical nuclear forces of NATO, many of which could reach the Soviet Union, should be included in the American total, and if so, should not the French and British strategic forces be similarly counted, and if these, why not also the approximately 700 IRBMs and MRBMs that the Soviet Union has targeted on Western Europe and the Warsaw Treaty Organization's own tactical nuclear forces.[3]

As these problems illustrate, SALT agreements will be difficult

[2] The initial American and Soviet proposals are described in *New York Times,* August 1, 1970 and January 17, 1971. The United States first proposed that ABMs be banned or limited to the defense of national capitals. For the later proposal that a limited number of ABMs might be deployed either for the defense of national capitals or for ICBM fields, see *New York Times,* July 23, 1971.

[3] See *ibid.,* February 4, 1971.

to negotiate, even with the best of good will and endeavor. This chapter starts with a description of the consequences that would follow a failure to reach any agreement; consequences first for the Soviet-American strategic balance and then for European security arrangements. Once these consequences have been outlined, the chapter considers how they might be modified as a result of an agreement to one or another of the two initial proposals described above. Although the chapter does not consider possible compromises between the initial American and Soviet proposals, the analysis will provide a baseline for judgment on such compromises, e.g., an agreement that essentially limits only ABMs and SS-9s.[4]

II

The deployment of MIRVs will produce the first major change in the present strategic environment. For the past decade, the reliability, accuracy, and warhead yield of ICBMs has been such that the firing of two, three, or in most instances many more missiles would have been required to insure the almost certain destruction of a single enemy missile, provided it was in a hardened silo. Under these circumstances, it was possible for each superpower to have a land-based, fixed-site, hardened ICBM force that could ride out a first strike from the ICBMs of the other and still have sufficient missiles remaining to achieve its desired "assured destruction" of the enemy's people and industry in a second strike. It was possible for this condition to prevail even in the absence of numerical equality in ICBMs, provided the numerically superior state's advantage in numbers of missiles (e.g., 2:1) fell short of the missile-kill ratio (e.g., 4:1) imposed by the technical characteristics of

[4] This chapter was prepared for press prior to the agreements reached in Moscow in May 1972 at the end of the first phase of the SALT negotiations. For the content of these agreements, see *Survival*, July–August 1972, pp. 188–99. So far as their general consequence for the strategic balance and European security arrangements are concerned, the terms of the Moscow agreements are substantially no different in their effect than the proposals considered in this chapter, and the chapter's consideration of the first alternative (no agreement at all) still provides the best measure for assessing the import of SALT Phase I.

its missiles, and provided the absolute number of missiles remaining to the inferior power was still sufficient to achieve "assured destruction."

But with missiles carrying MIRVs it will be possible in time for one ICBM to destroy more than one enemy missile. American defense officials have already expressed the concern that by the mid-1970s—given certain assumptions about improved missile accuracy, reliability, and retargeting capability—some 420 Soviet SS-9 ICBMs (each with three individually guided 5-megaton warheads) could destroy approximately 95 percent of America's 1000 Minuteman missiles in their present configuration. Indeed, given the same performance assumptions, the Soviet Union could produce a comparable effect with their present force of some 300 SS-9s, provided each carried six 2-MT warheads. In the absence of offsetting measures, then, the advent of MIRV, together with expected improvements in accuracy, reliability, and retargeting, promises to change Minuteman from an "invulnerable deterrent" to a sunken duck.[5]

---

[5] For the estimate of 420 SS-9 missiles, see the testimony of Secretary of Defense Melvin Laird and John S. Foster, Director of Defense Research and Engineering, in House of Representatives Committee on Appropriations Subcommittees, *Hearings, Safeguard Antiballistic Missile System,* 91st Cong., 1st Sess. (1969), pp. 9, 27; Senate Committee on Armed Services, *Hearings, Authorization for Military Procurement, Research and Development, Fiscal Year 1970, and Reserve Strength,* 91st Cong., 1st Sess. (1969) [hereafter cited as SCAS, *Hearings FY 1970 Budget*], pp. 1713–14; and Senate Committee on Foreign Relations, Subcommittee on Arms Control, International Law, and Organization *ABM, MIRV, SALT, and the Nuclear Arms Race,* 91st Cong., 2nd Sess. (1970) [hereafter cited as SCFR, *1970 ABM Hearings*], pp. 437, 512. The estimate assumed a .25 nautical-mile CEP and a .8 reliability. The testimony is not clear as to whether the .8 refers to overall reliability, to reprogrammable reliability, or to both. Subsequent calculations in this chapter assume the second case.

For American concern about the threat from 300 SS-9s with a six 2-MT MIRV configuration, see *New York Times,* February 27, 1971. A force of this order, given comparable technical assumptions, could destroy about 94 percent of the Minuteman force.

This and the later calculations in this chapter regarding the effect of various Soviet SS-9 forces (whatever the size and number of warheads) assume that the Soviet force has a .8 reprogrammable reliability; a .956 nonreprogrammable reliability; and a .25 nautical-mile CEP. The single-shot kill probabilities were read from the General Electric Missile Effectiveness Calculator, which is based on the following formulae (W = warhead yield in MT;

Similar worries no doubt plague the strategists in Moscow. The completion of the present MIRV program of the United States will equip its missiles with more than 7200 individually guided warheads. The yield of these warheads will, however, be considerably lower than those projected for the SS-9. Accordingly, given the same assumptions about accuracy, reliability, and retargeting ability, it is doubtful if this projected American force could destroy more than 80 percent of the present Soviet strength of some 1500 ICBMs. But there is nothing in the nature of the technology involved to prevent the United States from improving the accuracy of its missiles to the point where the presently configured Soviet ICBM force would fare no better than Minuteman in the event of an enemy first strike. Although the United States government has announced a halt in its program to achieve such accuracies, the American statement is bound to be less than totally reassuring to Soviet planners, and they must therefore confront the same kind of vulnerability problem toward the end of the decade that American planners fear they will meet in its middle.[6]

H = hardness in psi overpressure; L = lethal radius in nautical miles for targets between 50 and 1000 psi):

$$L = \frac{2.9W^{1/3}}{H^{.35}} \qquad SSKP = 1 - e^{-.69315} \left(\frac{L}{CEP} \right)^2$$

Unless otherwise noted, American ICBMs are assumed to be hardened to withstand 300 psi. On this point see Institute for Strategic Studies, *The Military Balance 1970–1971* (London: Institute for Strategic Studies, 1971), p. 90; and the statement by Senator Symington in SCAS, *Hearings FY 1970 Budget*, p. 1874.

The calculations in this chapter are the responsibility of Warner R. Schilling but the result of a joint effort with Professor Lynn E. Davis of Barnard College, whose collaboration in this part of the chapter's analysis is acknowledged with great pleasure. For the method used, see ORSA Ad Hoc Committee on Professional Standards, "Guidelines For the Practice of Operations Research," *Operations Research*, September 1971, pp. 1204–5; and Lynn E. Davis and Warner R. Schilling, "All You Ever Wanted to Know about MIRV and ICBM Calculations but Were Not Cleared to Ask," *Journal of Conflict Resolution*, June 1973.

[6] In December 1969, President Nixon assured Senator Edward Brooke that the administration had no programs to improve significantly the accuracies of its MIRVs and that funding for such a program had been canceled in the FY 1971 budget. See *New York Times*, April 23, 1970. See also the statement of

A vulnerability problem might have materialized in time, even without MIRV, as a result of improvements in the reliability, accuracy, and yield of missiles carrying only one warhead, since these improvements might in theory have reduced the missile-kill ratio to 1:1. But this limit would have been difficult to achieve, and at all events the effects of MIRV go far beyond improvements of this order. For as the American concerns noted above illustrate, MIRV can make feasible missile-kill ratios of 1:2 or 1:3 even in the absence of perfect missile reliability.

There are nine different ways the superpowers can consider meeting the prospective vulnerability of their present land-based, fixed-site, hardened ICBMs. These are (1) do nothing (leave their ICBM forces as they are and permit their vulnerability to increase); (2) abandon them (write off their ICBMs as obsolete and place their reliance on bombers and submarine-launched missiles);

John S. Foster in SCFR, *1970 ABM Hearings*, p. 509. President Nixon also has stressed his interest in avoiding weapons developments that the Soviet Union might interpret as threatening a disarming attack. See House of Representatives, *Foreign Policy Message from The President of the United States*, Document No. 92-53, 92nd Cong., 1st Sess. (1971) [hereafter cited as *The President: 1971 Foreign Policy Message*], pp. 131, 134.

But it may prove be difficult for the Soviet government to plan on the basis of these assurances as it would for the American government if the circumstances were reversed, especially if the administration's discussion of American policy continues to deal in ambiguous terms such as "hard-target capability" instead of specific CEPs. Moreover, some recent references are so studded with security deletions as to easily arouse the suspicions of a Soviet reader. See House of Representatives Committee on Armed Services, *Hearings on Military Posture*, 92nd Cong., 1st Sess. (1971) [hereafter cited as HCAS, *Hearings FY 1972 Budget*], pp. 3042, 3044–45.

The estimate of 80 percent is based on what might appear to be a "worst case" from the Soviet side: all American missiles were assumed to have the same reliabilities as were assigned to the SS-9 force in fn. 5; all of the Poseidon missiles were assumed available; and the following American CEPs and yields were assumed: Titan II, .50 nm and 10 MT; Minuteman II, .30 nm and 2 MT; Minuteman III, .25 nm and .2 MT; and Poseidon, .27 nm and .05 MT. All Soviet ICBMs were assumed to be hardened to 300 psi except the 220 SS-7s and SS-8s; of these, 140 were assumed to be soft targets and 80 hardened to 100 psi.

For a discussion of the present and potential American MIRV threat to the Soviet ICBM force that uses a range of assumptions, see Davis and Schilling, "All You Ever Wanted To Know about MIRV and ICBM Calculations but Were Not Cleared To Ask."

(3) multiply them (build additional missiles); (4) warn them (plan to fire missiles upon receiving radar warning that an attack is on the way, so that when enemy warheads arrive there are nothing left but holes in the ground); (5) fake them (build dummy missile silos, so that a large percentage of enemy warheads hit fake holes instead of real missiles); (6) hide them (camouflage missile sites, so that the enemy does not know their location); (7) superharden them (increase the blast resistance of silos, so that a much larger number of warheads will be required to destroy one missile); (8) move them (place missiles on trucks or railroad cars and keep them in motion or prepared to move on warning, so that the enemy will not know their exact location); or (9) defend them (with an ABM system).

The choices the superpowers make among these alternatives (which are not exclusive) will have very important arms control consequences. If they were to do nothing and thus permit their ICBMs to become increasingly vulnerable, the superpowers could place themselves under considerable strain to preempt during time of crisis. The extent of this strain would depend on each superpower's estimate of the difference that striking first at the other's ICBMs would make in the total amount of death and destruction it would suffer as a result of the war. Since the amount of damage a superpower would receive in a nuclear war is not directly proportionate to the number of warheads or the amount of megatonnage dropped on it (but is subject instead to the law of diminishing returns), this difference might not be great, provided each superpower had an assured capability of delivering, in any event, a very large number of warheads by submarines or bombers in its second strike.

A decision to do nothing about the vulnerability of ICBMs would, therefore, be accompanied by a decision to do a great deal about the quantity and quality of air- and ocean-based delivery systems. In order to insure that there would be no overall deterioration in their deterrent postures, both superpowers would take measures to add to their bomber forces or at least to upgrade their quality. The superpowers would also deploy more missiles in what now appears to be the safest environment, the oceans. The United

States, for example, would almost certainly deploy ULMS (the Undersea Long Range Missile System)—a submarine capable of launching more missiles than can the Polaris, from a greater depth, and from a much larger part of the ocean.

The incentive to augment bomber and submarine forces would be even greater if the superpowers should decide to react to MIRV by simply writing off their fixed-site ICBMs. This is not, however, a choice that either superpower is likely to make much before the end of the decade, if ever, because these forces are currently central to the strategic postures of both. It has been the policy of the United States to maintain three separate delivery systems (land-based missiles, sea-based missiles, and bombers) in sufficient strength that, in the event of the worst imaginable Soviet first strike, each would be capable of achieving the amount of assured destruction believed necessary to deter a Soviet attack.[7]

On its part, the Soviet Union would seem even less in a position to write off its ICBMs. As of mid-1971, these missiles represented a far larger share of the total Soviet strategic force than American ICBMs constituted of the American strategic force: some 75 percent of the Soviet delivery vehicles (cf. 50 percent for the United States); some 66 percent of Soviet warheads (cf. 32 percent); and possibly 76 percent of the total Soviet megatonnage (cf. 37 percent). The Soviet Union is therefore unlikely to consider abandoning its ICBMs until it has added greatly to its number of submarines and perhaps bombers, as well.[8]

[7] For recent instances of the American commitment to three independent deterrent systems, see *The President: 1971 Foreign Policy Message*, pp. 133–34, and John S. Foster's testimony in House of Representatives Committee on Armed Services, *Hearings on Military Posture*, 91st Cong., 2nd Sess. (1970) [hereafter cited as HCAS, *Hearings FY 1971 Budget*], Part 2, p. 7916.

On the American determination to deploy ULMS in the event that provisions cannot be made for the security of Minuteman, see Foster's testimony, *ibid.*, pp. 7916–17; and the views of Secretary Laird as reported in *New York Times*, March 21, 1971.

[8] These figures are derived from Institute for Strategic Studies, *The Military Balance 1971–1972* (London: Institute for Strategic Studies, 1971). The megatonnage figures assume that each Soviet bomber carries three 5-MT bombs and each American bomber four 2-MT bombs. Warhead percentages are for separately targetable warheads.

Even if the passage of time should find the United States more prepared to change its policy or the Soviet Union less dependent on land-based missiles for its deterrent force, the decision to dismantle its ICBMs is not a choice that either superpower would be willing to make unilaterally. However unattractive may be the vision of a world in which the ICBMs of both superpowers are vulnerable to a first strike, each superpower would probably find it preferable to a world in which the other had a large ICBM force and it did not. For in this event, the superpower which retained its ICBMs would have the potential for producing greater destruction on the territory of the other, and it would also have a greater capability for limited missile strikes, since submarine-launched missiles are less suitable for this mission. Accordingly, the only way the superpowers are likely to abandon their fixed-site ICBMs is through a negotiated agreement.

The difficulty with an agreement between the superpowers to abandon their ICBMs (assuming they were agreed that it would benefit their own relationship) is that it would deprive them of their most effective weapon against the future missiles of China. All points considered, then, the most likely future is one in which each superpower will retain a sizable land-based ICBM capability and search among the remaining seven alternatives for a way of decreasing the vulnerability of those missiles to the MIRVed forces of the other.[9]

If either superpower chooses the third alternative, deciding to add to the number of its land-based ICBMs, in order to decrease their vulnerability to a first strike, the effect will be to increase the

[9] For the communication problems involved in using SLBMs for limited, controlled exchanges, see Neville Brown, "Deterrence from the Sea," *Survival*, June 1970, pp. 194–98.

Unlike the United States, the Soviet Union could conceivably cover potential targets in China with IRBMs (as it already does for Western Europe). But this would require deploying many of the missiles close to the border, a security risk that the Soviet Union is unlikely to take. A more likely choice for the Soviet Union is to shorten the range of its ICBMs. The Soviet Union is reported to have already installed about 100 SS-11 ICBMs with a variable-range capability in its IRBM and MRBM fields for possible use against Western Europe. See Institute for Strategic Studies, *The Military Balance 1971–1972*, p. 5, and *New York Times*, February 11, 1970.

vulnerability of the other's forces. Since MIRV will permit missile-kill ratios of 1:N (where N > 1), the superpowers cannot achieve mutual security even in equality of numbers of missiles, and there will be less security (for one) in inequality. Moreover, a meaningful inequality would be difficult to achieve, for if the value of N is greater than one, the additional missiles built by one superpower could always be offset by the other's building a smaller number. The choice of "multiplication," then, would stimulate the arms race without any real prospect of decreasing the vulnerability of either superpower.

A different order of arms control problem is involved in the fourth alternative: placing ICBMs on a launch-on-warning status and firing them upon notice that an attack is underway. The deployment of a satellite warning system will provide notice of an attack within a few minutes of an enemy's launch, and the back-up provided by at least two shorter-ranged warning systems (the Ballistic Missile Early Warning System and over-the-horizon radar) would help to correct an erroneous alert by any one.[10] But a commitment to a launch-on-warning policy would place, for all practical purposes, the choice of war in the hands of machines and invite the risk of war by radar, sensor, or computer error. Although there is no publicly recorded instance of existing warning systems giving a false alarm that was not recognized as such within a few minutes, one cannot help but be impressed with the possibility of a first time.[11]

It would be feasible to extend the time available for correcting a false alarm by building into missiles either an "arming mechanism" that would need to be triggered from the ground before the missile

---

[10] The new 647 satellite system is expected to provide warning within a minute of the launching of either an ICBM or SLBM. See *New York Times*, November 7, 1970. Deployment of the Perimeter Acquisition Radar for Safeguard would provide a fourth warning system.

[11] Misleading radar warnings reportedly led to several false alerts in the late 1950s (see *New York Times*, April 19, 1958); radar reflections from the moon caused numerous false alerts in 1960–61 (*ibid.*, December 7, 1960, and February 5, 1962); and a communications failure with the Thule radar station led to a false alarm during the 1961 Berlin crisis (*ibid.*, April 1 and 4, 1962). A false alert also occurred in December 1950—during the Korean War—but this apparently was caused by a ground observer (*ibid.*, July 25, 1959).

reached its target, if the warheads were to explode, or a "destruct mechanism" that could be used to destroy the missile in flight if the alarm should prove false. Either arrangement, provided it could be operated well beyond the first few minutes after launch, might make possible sufficient time to be certain that the only alarms responded to were real ones, although each arrangement is open to sabotage. One superpower might be able to "spoof" the other's missiles out of their silos by a false alert and then leave the tricked power with the uncomfortable choice of starting the war or losing its missiles (thereby leaving it vulnerable to later black-mail). This would appear to be the kind of strategy, however, that comes more readily to the mind of a "defense intellectual" than to a real live politician. More serious is the certainty that both super-powers would have a strong incentive to try to devise ways whereby each could trigger the other's destruct mechanism or jam its arming mechanism so that in the event of war they would be able to reduce the damage to themselves. It would seem plausible, therefore, that if a superpower decided to introduce such mecha-nisms as part of a launch-on-warning posture, the power would en-deavor to keep it a closely guarded secret, if the power dared to do it at all.[12]

The next two options, faking and hiding, entail variants of the two arms control problems discussed above. Building "convincing" fake silos and missiles would probably cost so much that the temp-tation would be strong to build and install real ones. But even if the costs could be lowered, building a large number of fake missile

---

[12] At present, Minuteman is reported to be armed automatically, once it is well on its way, by the force of acceleration. See Joel Larus, *Nuclear Weapons Safety and the Common Defense* (Columbus: Ohio State University Press, 1967), p. 68. Presumably Minuteman already contains a destruct mechanism that can be activated shortly after launch, since there would otherwise be no way of destroying a missile that was erratically launched and en route to an American or allied city. But a mechanism that could be used only in the first few minutes of flight would not provide any significant amount of time to cor-rect for a false alert. For a puzzling exchange on this issue between Senator Symington and Secretary Laird, see Senate Committee on Foreign Relations, Subcommittee on International Organizations and Disarmament Affairs, *Hear-ings, Strategic and Foreign Policy Implications of ABM Systems*, 91st Cong., 1st Sess. (1969) [hereafter cited as SCFR, *1969 ABM Hearings*], pp. 207–10.

sites would bring the same multiplication problem as building real missiles, tor neither superpower could be certain that the other's good fakes were not real.

Present and prospective capabilities in satellite reconnaissance suggest that it would be extremely difficult to "hide" an ICBM. Since a hidden missile could afford to be in a non-hardened location, there would seem to be a wide variety of possible hiding places: barns, buildings, farm silos, etc. The problem would lie in the avoidance of detection during the process of getting the missile to the hiding place and in hiding the arrangements for its command and servicing. The publicity that might attend these activities in any built-up area would seem to restrict potential locations to less populated environments, at least in the United States, but it is in precisely these areas that any signs of untoward traffic would be most easily observed from above. Under the circumstances, the security of a hiding place would seem uncertain at the start and with the passage of time increasingly open to question. As a result, the pressure in time of crisis to launch such missiles on warning would be great. The development of a reliable "dormant" missile —one that could be left unserviced for a long period of time and fired by remote control—might make for more confident hiding, but here the firing signal might be more vulnerable to electromagnetic jamming and again the incentive to fire on warning would be strong.[13]

The difficulty with superhardening silos as a way of decreasing the vulnerability of fixed-site ICBMs is that this measure can be offset by further improvements in the accuracy of enemy missiles. A tenfold increase in the resistance of a silo (e.g., from 300 pounds per square inch to 3000 pounds per square inch) could be offset by a reduction of a little more than half in the CEP (circular error probable) of the attacking missile (e.g., from 0.25 nautical miles to 0.12 nautical miles). Moreover, the construction of silos with resistances on the order of 3000 psi would be very expensive and possi-

[13] Considerations of this order, together with maintenance and sabotage problems, led to rejection of such a missile system in the Pentagon's Strat-X Project, which surveyed land-based systems which could supersede Minuteman. See *New York Times*, July 17, 1967.

ble only in special geological environments. The combination of expense and potential obsolescence appears to have led the United States to decide not to implement its hard-rock silo program.[14]

The effectiveness of an intermediate increase in hardness (e.g., from 300 psi to 900 psi) depends, of course, on the character of the assumed threat. The recently announced program of the United States to triple the hardness of its silos for Minuteman III would appear to have limited utility against the kind of SS-9 threat the Department of Defense has previously projected (some 420 SS-9s, each with three 5MT warheads and a 0.25 nautical mile CEP), although the program could have other advantages. It would serve to offset expected improvements in the accuracy of the SS-11 and perhaps to increase the effectiveness of an ABM defense for Minuteman. Intermediate hardening could ensure the survival of a significant number of Minutemen, as noted later in this chapter, if the program were extended to all 1000 silos and the Soviet SS-9 force was limited to a smaller number of missiles (e.g., 300). The effectiveness of the program, however, could be offset by a reduction in the Soviet CEP from 0.25 nautical miles to 0.16 nautical miles (i.e., from 1500 feet to about 970 feet).[15]

The Soviet Union would have somewhat more to gain than the United States from a policy of hardening to the order of 1000 psi, since the American MIRVs will have smaller warheads than those

[14] For military and geological problems entailed in the hard-rock program, see HCAS, *Hearings FY 1971 Budget*, p. 7118; SCFR, *1969 ABM Hearings*, p. 286. For an estimate that the program would have cost $5–$7 billion and the announcement of the decision to abandon the program, see *New York Times*, August 26, 1970.

[15] The American program is reported to cost between $500 million and $1 billion and is designed to increase the resistance of Minuteman III silos from 300 to 900 psi. See *New York Times*, December 6, 1970. For suggestions that hardening can contribute to the effectiveness of an ABM defense, see SCAS, *Hearings FY 1970 Budget*, p. 229, and *Hearings FY 1971 Budget*, p. 1181.

Given the new program, a force of 420 SS-9 missiles with the characteristics previously assumed could still destroy some 89 percent of the Minuteman force (leaving about 111 missiles and 287 warheads), and the program would have cost $8–$17 million per missile saved.

Against a force of 420 SS-9s it would not make much sense to extend the program to all 1000 silos, for this would result in saving only 49 more warheads. For the case of a force of 300 SS-9s, see footnote 50.

the Soviet Union is expected to deploy. Hardening to this level would prolong the security of Soviet missiles when American CEPs began to drop below 1500 feet, but once CEPs narrowed to about 600 feet, the Soviet program would cease to provide any real protection for its ICBMs. In short, the choice of increased hardening (whether super- or intermediate) would prove to be a short-run palliative for both superpowers against the kind of CEPs that may be available by the end of the decade.

The most evident problems with the eighth alternative—substituting mobile, land-based missiles for fixed-site ICBMs—are cost and vulnerability. Even with the assumption that the present missiles could be removed from their silos and placed on their new carriers, the costs would be high. The carriers would have to be built along with new navigation, command-and-control, and other supporting systems. It is not feasible to estimate these costs from the public record, but it may be relevant to note that for Minuteman I and II the total cost of the supporting systems was about $8 billion. The new carriers would no doubt cost less than Minuteman silos, but it would appear to be cheaper to navigate, command, and service a fixed-site missile than a mobile one.[16]

Mobile missiles would be soft targets and open to destruction by even crudely aimed warheads, provided a sufficient number were distributed near their last known location. This point would become critical if satellite reconnaissance reached the state where an attacking power could know the location of the enemy's mobile missiles at the time when it launched its attack. In this event, a rail-mobile system would appear to be quite vulnerable, since the destruction of a train carrying the missile(s) would require the production of a low amount of blast pressure along only some 50 linear miles of track. A truck-mobile system confined to special roads would be equally vulnerable. A truck or ground-effect machine

---

[16] When Secretary McNamara canceled the rail-mobile Minuteman program in 1961, he estimated that a rail-mobile Minuteman would cost 50–60 percent more than a fixed-site Minuteman. See Senate Committee on Armed Services, *Hearings, Military Procurement Authorization Fiscal Year 1962*, 87th Cong., 1st Sess. (1961), p. 33. The estimate of supporting costs for Minuteman is based on a letter to the editor by Albert Wohlstetter in *New York Times*, June 29, 1969.

that could travel in any direction over open terrain would be much more difficult to destroy, since its area of potential movement would be greatly increased, but the cost of special carriers of this sort would be far greater than that of trains or more conventionally wheeled trucks.[17]

The high costs and the difficult command-and-control and support problems associated with a fully mobile land-based missile system may account for the interest of the United States in a more limited but presumably less expensive land-mobile system: the shelter-based Minuteman. Under this program, upon warning of an incoming attack, a truck would carry the missile a few miles away to any one of a number of shelters or garages located in a circle around the missile's initial position. The advantage of pre-positioned shelters, which would be hardened to provide some blast protection, is that they would simplify the provision of supporting and command-and-control systems, and since the Soviet Union would not know which shelter would contain the missile, all of the shelters would have to be attacked to insure the missile's destruction.[18]

For this system to work, the number of shelters must exceed the number of shelter-effective warheads available to the attacking power, and if the system is to be competitive, the total cost of building a shelter (including supporting systems) must be lower than the cost to an opponent of adding an effective warhead to its striking force. The second condition would appear to be easily met. But to meet the first, if the Soviet Union could, as reported, fit each SS-9 with 18 200KT warheads, the United States might end up building as many as ten shelters per missile, which would clearly require a multibillion-dollar program.[19]

---

[17] For one mobile-system program under consideration the research and development costs alone have been estimated at $1 billion, and John S. Foster has implied that a mobile system could cost as much as the hard-rock silo program. See SCAS, *Hearings FY 1971 Budget*, p. 1182, and SCAS, *Hearings FY 1970 Budget*, pp. 214–15, 1792.

[18] For a description of this system, see HCAS, *Hearings FY 1971 Budget*, p. 7916, and *New York Times*, January 7, 1970.

[19] Shelters of course could be added to the circle as needed, but five shelters per Minuteman (as implied in the *New York Times* report above) might

The most consequential point for arms control is that the deployment of a shelter system would also constitute an implementation of the "faking" alternative. For if one superpower built shelters, there would be no way for the other to tell whether some or all of the shelters did not contain additional missiles. Accordingly, the deployment of shelters could provide the same stimulus to the arms race as would the multiplication alternative.[20]

The burden of the discussion of the preceding alternatives is that, if a superpower is intent on reducing the vulnerability of its fixed-site ICBMs, there is much to recommend a close consideration of the ninth and final alternative: to defend them with an ABM system. The "defend" choice starts with the possible economic advantage of building on an existing deterrent (as compared to the construction of a whole new mobile force), is more easily upgraded to offset increases in the accuracy or number of attacking warheads than a hardening program (it would be feasible to add more Sprints to defend a Minuteman but not to add more concrete), and avoids the arms control problems involved in multiplying, warning, faking, or hiding.

This ninth alternative is, of course, a choice that the United States made with the Safeguard program. The military effectiveness of this program was, however, questioned on two major counts: it would not work as well as expected, and even if it did, it could be easily overwhelmed by additions to the Soviet attacking force. Neither criticism can be readily assessed on the basis of the public record. Given the complexity of the components of an ABM

---

be insufficient. A warhead capability of 18 200KT frequently has been assigned the SS-9 (see, e.g., *New York Times*, April 14, 1969). If these warheads had the same accuracy and reliability expected for the 3 5MT configuration, 420 SS-9s could destroy 85 percent of a 1000-Minuteman force in a five-shelter arrangement, but only 52 percent in a ten-shelter arrangement, assuming a 50 psi shelter.

If the total unit cost of a shelter (research and development, construction, provision for command and control, etc.) ran as high as $500,000, a ten-shelter arrangement for 500 Minutemen would cost about $2.5 billion.

[20] This problem might be avoided if the top of the shelters could be opened occasionally to permit satellite reconnaissance. A more reliable approach to the problem would be to permit the Soviets to inspect the shelters at times of their choosing.

system (radars, missiles, computers, and computer programs) and the fact that they can never be fully tried before the event, the actual performance of the system in combat would be difficult to predict with confidence, even on the basis of classified information. But uncertainty about performance cuts two ways. It can also reduce the confidence of an attacking power (whose offensive systems are similarly complex and untried) that militarily significant gains can be achieved from a first strike, which is the object of defense in the first place.

The validity of the second criticism would appear to be the more consequential issue: whether, given comparable assumptions about technical performance of both offensive and defensive systems, the costs to the defender of a successful intercept are greater than the costs to the attacker of adding an effective warhead to its attacking force. Since the United States has not revealed its estimate of the first and the Soviet Union has not provided its estimate of the second, an independent judgment is not easily reached. The Department of Defense claimed in 1969 that with the full deployment of the Safeguard system these costs would be about even, but the reasoning behind this estimate is not apparent. That the Department later expected intercept costs to be quite high in relation to the expected costs of an offsetting warhead can be inferred from its subsequent interest in supplementing the Safeguard program with the Hardsite defense system, which would defend Minuteman with cheaper radars and perhaps cheaper missiles than those employed in Safeguard.[21]

Ironically, the more effective an ABM defense appears to be in

[21] The 1969 estimate was made by John S. Foster; see SCAS, *Hearings FY 1970 Budget,* pp. 224–225. His unit cost for each attacking warhead seems most arbitrary, and his unit cost for each defending warhead appears too low. On this last point, compare Abram Chayes and Jerome B. Wiesner, *ABM: An Evaluation of the Decision to Deploy an Antiballistic Missile System* (New York: Harper and Row, 1969), pp. 87, 90n.

On the growing interest in supplementing Safeguard with a hardsite defense, see HCAS, *Hearings FY 1971 Budget,* pp. 7950, 8301, 8329–8330. An excellent discussion, con and pro, of the military and political issues involved in an ABM defense for Minuteman can be found in the testimony of Wolfgang Panofsky and Albert Wohlstetter in SCAS, *Hearings FY 1971 Budget,* Part 3, pp. 2211–2415.

meeting the MIRV threat to fixed-site ICBMs, the greater its potential for introducing a whole new strategic instability: that which would come from the deployment of an ABM system to defend cities. An ABM defense for ICBMs is, of course, inherently more feasible than one for cities. A defense that could "save" 40 percent of its ICBMs could be judged a success; the same cannot be said for a defense for cities. Moreover, cities are bigger and softer targets than hardened missiles, and a city defense therefore must cover a larger area and intercept at a greater distance from the target (which complicates the task of distinguishing between warheads and decoys).

It is therefore quite possible for a superpower to decide that an ABM defense for missiles would be economical but that one for cities would not. The difficulty, from the standpoint of arms control, is whether a choice of this kind would be clear to the other superpower. What gives the American Safeguard program its "no-cities" face is the plan to group the terminal defense systems around missile and bomber bases, not cities (except for Washington). But there is no way the United States can avoid gaining experience in the construction and operation of the components of a city defense, since Safeguard uses the same components earlier designed for a city-defense system. In addition, the area-defense components of Safeguard would lend themselves just as readily to city as to Minuteman and bomber defense. There are, then, grounds on which Soviet military planners could argue that the Safeguard program did not demonstrate that the United States had decided conclusively against the deployment of an ABM system for city defense.[22]

The key point for arms control is that, if one superpower should appear to the other to be deploying an ABM system for city defense, the effect on the stability of the balance of terror would be almost as great as that from MIRV. If a superpower can couple a large counterforce capability (which MIRV makes possible) with an extensive city defense, it can confront its opponent with the prospect of very asymmetrical destruction in the event of war. This

[22] The city-defense potential of Safeguard can not be judged fully until more is known about the location of the radars and missiles to be deployed for the protection of bomber bases.

asymmetry is possible, however, only if the other superpower does not make a determined effort to offset its opponent's defensive system. Accordingly, if one superpower should appear to move in the direction of an ABM system for city defense, the other would certainly respond with large increases in its offensive forces and probably with a deployment of an ABM system to cover its own cities as well.[23]

To summarize this discussion of the nine alternative ways in which the superpowers can react to the vulnerability that MIRV will bring to their fixed-site ICBMs, it is apparent that there are no wholly satisfactory answers to the problem of vulnerability. A choice of any one of the nine alternatives would entail some undesirable political or military consequences.

Three points follow from this condition. The first is that neither superpower is likely to respond to MIRV by choosing only one of these alternatives. In both governments, the undesirable features of any one alternative will produce uncertainty and division about the most sensible course of action, and moved both by the need for internal political-bureaucratic accommodation and by an interest in keeping their options open, the superpowers will probably decide on policies which embrace a number of the alternatives. This tendency toward a mixed response can already be seen in the United States, where the defend choice has been coupled with a hardening program without at the same time reducing interest in a shelter-based system or diminishing pressure for upgrading sea and bomber forces.[24]

---

[23] The possible asymmetries are striking. In 1968 Secretary McNamara estimated that a nuclear war in 1975 (given the strategic forces that the superpowers were expected to have by that date) could result in 10 million American fatalities (about 4 percent of the population) and 80 million Soviet fatalities (about 30 percent of the population), provided the United States struck first and provided the United States had built an ABM system for city defense, the cost of which he estimated to be between $22 billion and $40 billion. The same calculations, however, indicated that if the Soviet Union had MIRVed its missiles by 1975, American fatalities would rise to 40 million, and if the Soviets also had built 550 mobile ICBMs, American fatalities would rise to 90 million. See House of Representatives Committee on Armed Services, *Hearings on Military Posture*, 90th Cong., 2nd Sess. (1968), pp. 8510–11.

[24] Thus for the FY 1971 budget the Joint Chiefs of Staff recommended the full-scale development and deployment of the B-1 bomber, ULMS, hard-rock

The second point is that the responses of the superpowers to the MIRV threat will probably not be parallel. As previously noted, an intermediate hardening program would make more sense during the next decade for the Soviet Union than for the United States. Similarly, the Soviet Union's prior experience with land-mobile IRBMs and the fact that it may already have developed a land-mobile ICBM, together with a greater confidence in the ability of Soviet society to insure secrecy of location and movement, could make the land-mobile system a more attractive choice to Soviet than to American planners.[25] Moreover, if the Soviet Union should add land-mobile ICBMs to its armory without subtracting a militarily equivalent number of fixed-site ICBMs, it would have employed the multiplication as well as the mobility option. Significant additions to the Soviet delivery forces are a certainty in any event, since the American deployment of MIRV will provide whatever additional incentive the Soviet Union may have needed to vastly expand its Polaris-type submarine fleet.

Another example of nonparallel response is provided by the possibility that the Soviet Union is not in a position to follow the American Safeguard precedent. Soviet ABM technology may not be effective enough to provide the necessary protection for fixed-site missiles. In 1968 and in 1969, the Department of Defense stated that the Galosh system appeared to be technically on a par with a system the United States had judged not worth deploying in 1961. Little work has been done on the Galosh system in recent years, and there has been no suggestion that it includes a Sprint-type missile for hard-point defense. Pending an improvement in their ABM technology, the Soviets might decide to counter the MIRVed forces of the United States by adding to their land-based missiles or placing a large number of them on a launch-on-warning status. This last alternative may appear less disturbing to Soviet of-

silos, *and* an advanced ICBM. SCAS, *Hearings FY 1971 Budget*, Part 1, p. 101.

[25] This obviously was Secretary McNamara's assumption; see fn. 23. The Soviet development of a mobile ICBM is discussed by Thomas W. Wolfe in House of Representatives Committee on Foreign Affairs, Subcommittee on National Security Policy and Scientific Developments, *Hearings, Diplomatic and Strategic Impact of Multiple Warhead Missiles*, 91st Cong., 1st Sess. (1969) [hereafter cited as HCFR, *1969 MIRV Hearings*], pp. 141, 144n.

ficials than to many American officials, because the Soviet Union may have relied on it before to offset American superiority. Since there is a dearth of public information on the sophistication of Soviet warning and command-and-control systems, it is difficult to assay the consequences of such a Soviet posture, but it could hardly be counted a net gain in arms control.[26]

Alternatively, should Soviet ABM technology be more advanced than American officials have estimated, the Soviet Union might still choose to deploy an ABM system, including point-defense missiles, to protect cities rather than missile sites. It is possible that the Soviet Union could not deploy an ABM system that would have a "missile defense only" face to the United States, even if the Soviet Union wanted to, since Soviet bomber and missile bases may be much closer to their urban centers than is the case in the United States.[27]

These examples of possible mixed and nonparallel responses to the advent of MIRV lead to a third and final point: the superpowers are going to encounter continuing difficulty and uncertainty in interpreting the strategic intent behind each other's actions, and the opportunities for each to conclude that the other is engaged in something more than coping with the prospective vulnerability of its land-based deterrent will be legion.

III

Four general consequences for the Soviet-American strategic relationship will follow from the unrestricted deployment of the MIRV-ABM technology: (1) a major new round in Soviet-Ameri-

[26] For comparisons between the Galosh system and the American Nike-Zeus, see Secretary Clifford's testimony in SCAS, *Hearings FY 1970 Budget*, p. 28, and John S. Foster's testimony in Senate Committee on Armed Services, Preparedness Investigating Subcommittee, *Hearings, Status of U.S. Strategic Power*, 90th Cong., 2nd Sess. (1968) [hereafter cited as SCAS, *1968 Strategic Power Hearings*], p. 113.

For Soviet statements in the early 1960s implying an intention and capability to launch on warning, see Thomas W. Wolfe, *Soviet Strategy at the Crossroads*, RAND Memorandum RM-4085-PR, April 1964, pp. 63–68.

[27] See Herbert Scoville, Jr., *Toward a Strategic Arms Limitation Agreement* (New York: Carnegie Endowment for International Peace, 1970), p. 26.

can armaments competition, both qualitative and quantitative; (2) a greater difficulty on the part of the superpowers and their allies in reaching common estimates of the character of the military balance; (3) an increased strain toward preemptive action in the event of a crisis; and (4) a mounting interest in limited strategic-war doctrine. This section considers briefly each of these consequences, and the next section discusses the manner in which they are likely to affect future European security arrangements.

That the United States and the Soviet Union stand on the threshold of very large expenditures for new strategic weapons systems, both offensive and defensive, is clear from the discussion in the preceding section. It is important to note, however, that the next rounds in the strategic arms race will be fueled by more than just the character of the new weapons technology—the vulnerability that MIRV will bring to the present fixed-site ICBMs of the two superpowers, and the potential of city-oriented ABM systems to downgrade the effectiveness of the present second-strike capabilities of the two superpowers. Equally important as an impetus to the arms race will be the intellectual concepts that will guide each superpower in its determination of force requirements.

The concepts that guide Soviet force requirements remain as difficult as ever to ascertain. At this writing, for example, it is not clear whether the recent expansion in the number of Soviet missiles represents a determination to seek a balance that the United States and its allies will recognize as "parity" or an effort to achieve a strategically meaningful superiority over the United States. It is possible that Soviet elites themselves are divided on this choice and may indeed have avoided any formal decision on the issue, since the first condition would have to be achieved prior to the second in any event. It is worth noting, however, that if the Soviet Union had wanted to italicize its interest in stabilizing the arms race, it could have stopped digging holes when it reached exactly the number 1054.[28]

---

[28] On the other hand, a Soviet decision to stop at 1054 would have required their leaders to live more dangerously than American leaders have been prepared to live. The Soviet Union would have confronted this choice when the United States was still debating the desirability of an ABM for city de-

In the American case, attention needs to be drawn to three policy guidelines determining force goals in recent years: (1) the concept of the "greater than expected threat" (which lends itself all too readily to the acronym GET); (2) the policy of maintaining three separate delivery systems, each of which can survive a Soviet first strike and produce assured destruction upon the enemy (multiple assured destruction, or MAD); and (3) the interest in maintaining some semblance of a war-fighting, damage-limiting posture (capability of firing first if necessary, or COFFIN). Each of these policy guidelines has been developed to meet a real and important strategic problem, but in application each has brought with it very significant arms control problems as well.

As a result of the application of GET, American forces are designed to meet the worst contingencies that can be imagined, i.e., the Soviets are expected to be preparing for a first strike, they are expected to build everything Americans think they are capable of building, and all Soviet weapons are assumed to perform in excess of the capabilities Americans expect them to have. Thus, in the spring of 1967, Secretary McNamara asserted that in his best judgment the Soviets were deploying an ABM system which was limited to the Moscow area and which was technically so unsophisticated that it would be militarily ineffective. Nonetheless, he went on to recommend to Congress the present American MIRV program, which, he stated, was designed to meet the contingency that the Soviets might deploy an ABM system far better than the one he thought they had and would deploy it throughout the whole of the Soviet Union.[29]

---

fense. Moreover, given the kind of CEPs Americans were anticipating, Soviet planners could have anticipated an American capability in the mid-1970s of destroying 80 to 90 percent of their land-based ICBMs. If this consideration weighed in the Soviet decision to continue deploying ICBMs, the Soviet Union has already employed the multiplication option.

The estimate of 90 percent is based on the assumptions described in fn. 6. For the 80 percent estimate (which is based on what are probably more realistic assumptions about yields, CEPs, and the use of SLBMs), see Davis and Schilling, "All You Ever Wanted to Know about MIRV and ICBM Calculations but Were Not Cleared to Ask."

[29] On the development of GET as a planning concept and its application in Soviet ABM deployment, see Secretary McNamara's testimony in House of

The military rationale for GET is, of course, the uncertainty that must attend any estimate of the Soviet Union's plans for its own strategic forces and the necessity, given the lead times required for the development and procurement of weapons, to prepare for the "worst" in order to avoid the possibility of experiencing it. The difficulty, so far as arms control is concerned, lies in the fact that weapons developments begun out of worries about the "worst" future continue to be deployed after a "better" future has in fact materialized. Thus, the missile programs laid down at the end of the Eisenhower administration and the beginning of the Kennedy administration out of fear of the "missile gap" were never canceled after the gap was shown by American intelligence to have been a false one. Similarly, in 1968 and later years, when American intelligence provided additional information supporting McNamara's original assessment of the Soviet ABM program, there was no corresponding reduction in the offsetting American MIRV program.

MAD is also addressed to a sensible strategic purpose: the desire to complicate the offensive and defensive preparations of the Soviet Union by confronting it with three different delivery systems and thereby to insure that assured destruction is certain and that Soviet leaders know it.[30] MAD, like GET, reflects the maxim that it is better to be safe than sorry, and both appear to assume that security is synonymous with more rather than fewer arms. But in building three different systems, *each* capable of producing assured

Representatives Committee on Armed Services, *Hearings on Military Posture*, 90th Cong., 1st Sess. (1967) [hereafter cited as HCAS, *Hearings FY 1968 Budget*], pp. 427, 429–30, 466; and Senate Committee on Armed Services and Senate Committee on Appropriations, Subcommittee on Department of Defense, *Hearings, Military Procurement Authorizations for Fiscal Year 1968*, 90th Cong., 1st Sess. (1967) [hereafter cited as SCAS, *Hearings FY 1968 Budget*], pp. 260, 284. For the criteria used in GET, see also the testimony of Alain C. Enthoven, SCAS, *1968 Strategic Power Hearings*, pp. 142–43, 145, 150.

[30] For statements by Deputy Secretary of Defense Paul H. Nitze, John S. Foster, and Gen. John D. Ryan, Chief of Staff, U.S. Air Force, illustrating respectively the capability, policy, and rationale of MAD, see Joint Committee on Atomic Energy, Subcommittee on Military Applications, *Hearings, Scope, Magnitude, and Implications of the United States Antiballistic Missile Program*, 90th Cong., 1st Sess. (1967), p. 49; and HCAS, *Hearings FY 1972 Budget*, pp. 2745, 2781.

destruction (and even this is a conservative estimate, since the effects of fallout and firestorms are not included in the damage estimates), the United States has failed to recognize that additional weapons do not necessarily provide additional security. On the contrary, excessive defensive preparations may serve only to stimulate Soviet fears and to fuel the arms race. This prospect would appear even more likely in the 1970s when, with the introduction of MIRV, one power's MAD may look like COFFIN to the other.

The American interest in having some capability of firing first if necessary (COFFIN) is similarly the result of a real policy problem: the American commitment to respond to a Soviet attack on Western Europe, if all other means fail, with the use of strategic nuclear weapons, and the belief that both the credibility and the discharge of this commitment require a counterforce, damage-limiting capability vis-à-vis the Soviet Union. For the most part, the forces for COFFIN have been provided out of the "surplus" of weapons (over those required for assured destruction) that have been generated through the application of GET and MAD. It is clear, however, that on occasion forces have been budgeted with counterforce needs explicitly in mind. Thus, while the present American MIRV program was justified in 1967 as a means of offsetting a greater-than-expected heavy Soviet ABM system, there are enough statements on the record to support the conclusion that an additional and antecedent reason for the development of this MIRV program was the desire to retain a counterforce capability in face of the expected increase in the number of land-based Soviet ICBMs.[31]

[31] On the development of MIRV, see SCFR, *1969 ABM Hearings,* pp. 200–201; HCAS, *Hearings FY 1972 Budget,* p. 2788; HCFR, *1969 MIRV Hearings,* pp. 11–12; and SCAS, *1968 Strategic Power Hearings,* pp. 9, 17, 26, 35, 147–48, 243, 283. For the use of the "surplus" from GET to provide forces for damage-limitation, see source last cited, pp. 118, 140.

For the military interest in a credible preemptive-threat capability and its association with the NATO commitment, see the testimony of Gen. Earle G. Wheeler, Chairman, Joint Chiefs of Staff, in SCAS, *Hearings FY 1968 Budget,* pp. 250–52; HCAS, *Hearings FY 1968 Budget,* pp. 424–25; and SCAS, *1968 Strategic Power Hearings,* p. 37; see also Gen. Thomas S. Power, *Design for Survival* (New York: Pocket Books, Inc., 1965), pp. 68, 123, 177; and Gen.

As a result of the application of these three policy guidelines, the United States developed in the early and mid-1960s a considerable numerical superiority over the Soviet Union in deliverable warheads. This superiority was not without its rationale, as noted above, or even without its uses (in the Cuban missile crisis, superiority may have contributed to the unwillingness of the Soviet Union to counter American pressures in the Caribbean with their own on West Berlin). But the pursuit of superiority has also served to stimulate the arms race and strain Soviet-American relations (witness the rapid increase in Soviet ICBMs since 1966 and, perhaps, the emplacement of missiles in Cuba in the first place) and has thereby made deterrence both more expensive and potentially more precarious.

The American pursuit of superiority was never pushed to the point where the United States had a highly effective damage-limiting capability, at least not against the kind of strategic forces the Soviet Union began to deploy after 1966. Given the ineffectiveness of ASW (anti-submarine warfare) technology, among other factors, a capability of this order would have required the deployment of ABMs for city defense. Secretary McNamara repeatedly advised against such a program on the grounds that the Soviet Union would only add to its offensive forces whatever was needed to offset the American ABM. The final position of the Johnson administration on this choice was blurred, since the program authorized, Sentinel, did have the potential for expansion to provide for a heavy city defense, and there were many, reportedly including the Joint Chiefs, who supported Sentinel for this reason.[32]

Curtis E. LeMay with Maj. Gen. Dale O. Smith, *America is in Danger* (New York: Funk and Wagnalls, 1968), pp. 63, 151.

The last two administrations of course have finessed the issue. They have neither renounced the threat to use strategic weapons in defense of Western Europe nor provided all the forces the Chiefs have considered necessary to back up that threat. Thus Secretary McNamara spoke in 1968 of the need for "the image of power superiority." See HCAS, *Hearings FY 1968 Budget*, p. 448.

[32] See Alain C. Enthoven and K. Wayne Smith, *How Much is Enough?* (New York: Harper and Row, 1971), pp. 188–89, 193; and statement by Gen. Wheeler, SCAS, *1968 Strategic Power Hearings*, p. 11.

The point of this brief review of past policies is to stress that future developments in the strategic arms race will be as sensitive to changes or continuities in strategic concepts as they will be to changes in military technology or to agreements reached or not reached at SALT. At present, American doctrine is in a state of flux. The Nixon administration has demonstrated by both word and deed that it is prepared to accept the new strategic balance occasioned by the great growth in Soviet strategic forces since 1966. Both the shift from Sentinel to Safeguard and the cancellation of a program designed to improve the accuracy of American MIRVs have been described as efforts to persuade the Soviet Union that the United States is not intent on offsetting the new Soviet offensive strength with major programs for damage limitation. The doctrine of "sufficiency" has been explicitly designed to symbolize the American acceptance of "equality" in strategic forces, and the willingness not to contest this new relationship is further evidenced by the administration's SALT proposal providing for parity in the total number of strategic delivery vehicles.[33]

But the doctrine of sufficiency does not mean that the United States has lost interest in maintaining a counterforce capability; on this point President Nixon has been perfectly clear. Nor is the American proposal for equality in delivery vehicles incompatible with COFFIN—if not against all Soviet missiles, at least against some. Since the key strategic relationship is the ratio of one power's warheads to the other's delivery vehicles, not the ratio of vehicles to vehicles, the effect of a parity agreement coupled with MIRV is better described as a condition of "mutual superiority" than as one of strategic equality.[34]

When this point is added to the fact that the Nixon administration appears as committed to planning on the basis of GET and MAD as was the Johnson administration, it is evident that the

[33] See *The President: 1971 Foreign Policy Message*, pp. 131–32; statement by Secretary Laird, HCAS, *Hearings FY 1972 Budget*, pp. 2367, 2563; text of President Nixon's announcement of the Safeguard program in *New York Times*, March 15, 1969; and fn. 6.

[34] On President Nixon's interest in having something more than an assured destruction capability, see *The President: 1971 Foreign Policy Message*, p. 131; and *New York Times*, February 26, 1971.

combination of American (or, for that matter, Soviet) planning concepts and continuing innovations in weapons technology has lost little of its explosive effect on the future course of the arms race. As the superpowers deploy their MIRVs and implement their mixed and nonparallel policies for coping with the vulnerability of their ICBMs, each will have ample opportunity to see greater-than-expected threats in the actions of the other and to interpret the consequent overinsurance of the delivery forces by one as signaling a secret ambition to jeopardize the assured-destruction capability of the other.

In the absence, then, of a comprehensive agreement from SALT, there is no reason to expect the strategic arms competition of the 1970s to be any less vigorous or expensive than that of the 1960s. Indeed, in the climate of suspicion that would inevitably follow the failure to secure an agreement from SALT, expenditures for strategic weapons would certainly increase. Thus as Soviet policy began to react more fully to the MIRV programs of the United States, American policy would react in turn. The mid-1970s would see at least a major expansion in the American ABM system to cover all the Minuteman fields and bomber bases, more expensive bomber-alert and -upgrading programs, and a decision to offset possible improvements in ASW by the deployment of ULMs. By the end of the decade, the superpowers might well be developing city-defense systems, and with each superpower having so many of its military eyes, ears, and brains in inner space, it would be remarkable if both were not engaged in expensive programs for satellite defense and offense.[35]

The second feature of a decade of unrestricted arms competition would be increased uncertainty regarding the nature of the military balance. Even if the superpowers should in time reach some discernible plateau of deployment of the new weapons systems (either by agreement, the pressure of other budgetary commitments, or a mutual willingness to live with about what each then has), it would still be very difficult for both powers to develop either a confident or a common picture of who can do what to whom.

[35] See the testimony of Harold A. Linstone in HCFA, *Science and Strategy*, p. 46.

The range of uncertainty regarding such matters as missile reliability, MIRV accuracy, the performance of radars and computers, the effectiveness of ASW measures, penetration aids, and ABM systems under heavy attack, and the effects of phenomena which in the absence of atmospheric testing will remain only partially understood (such as radar blackout and electrical magnetic pulse) will permit a wide variety of informed judgments on the question of just what would happen in the event of war. There would be, for example, ample opportunity for rather large divergencies among the following four judgments: A's conception of what A can do to B; B's conception of what A can do to B; A's conception of what B's conception is of what A can do to B; and B's conception of what A's conception is of what A can do to B.

How consequential divergent judgments of this order would prove would depend, of course, on the extent and direction of the divergencies. The possibility that in a crisis each superpower might believe that the other's reading of the military balance would lead it to blink first may be the most disturbing prospect, but it hardly exhausts the number of possible combinations among such judgments.

A third feature would be a greater strain toward preemption in time of crisis. How great a strain the MIRV-ABM technology will place on the superpowers to take preemptive action when resort to nuclear weapons seems imminent will partly turn on the manner in which the powers decide to respond to the vulnerability of their land-based missiles. The strain toward preemption depends on how large a difference in destruction a power may expect to incur as a result of striking first or second. If a power expects its opponent to fire on warning, for example, there is obviously little possibility of reducing destruction by firing first. But if both powers try to maintain a slow second-strike capability (one that fires only after being hit), the future size and vulnerability of bomber- and submarine-delivery systems may be critical. If both powers believe that no matter how vulnerable MIRV may make their land-based missiles, they will always retain sufficient strength in the air or at sea to deliver their conception of assured destruction and to prevent asymmetrical destruction, the strain toward preemption will be minimal. Given the proportion of each superpower's megatonnage currently carried by land-based missiles, the second condition would be difficult to achieve without substantial additions to present air- and sea-based forces, at least by the Soviet Union. Moreover, one or both superpowers could downgrade the effectiveness of these forces by adding to their air and missile defenses. And if developments in ASW should increase the vulnerability of submarine-launched missiles, it could become a very trigger-quick world indeed, for a submarine that is vulnerable to attack is unlikely to have even the opportunity to launch on warning.

A fourth consequence of the MIRV-ABM technology will be increased interest on the part of both superpowers in a variety of counterforce doctrines, including limited and controlled strategic exchanges. As the weapons systems that have been discussed here come into deployment in the mid-1970s, neither superpower is likely to find itself with the kind of counterforce capability that would permit it to undertake a first strike in the anticipation that it would escape with no more than high World War II–type casualties. Nonetheless, both powers will have vastly augmented their counterforce capabilities, and in an era of mounting warhead plenty it would be surprising if military planners on both sides did not turn their attention to new strategies for the employment of those warheads.

Other components of the new technology will also lend themselves to limited strategic exchanges. The complex of satellite surveillance, ground radars, and computer and display technology will make it relatively easy to identify whether few or many missiles are being fired. Moreover, technology that will permit a country to know where warheads are going (for purposes of ballistic-missile defense) is probably capable of permitting a country to know from where warheads have come. Technology of this sort, in addition to easing fears about third-power "catalytic" initiatives, would also bring an end to the "empty-hole" problem and thus make for far greater economy in the allocation of counterforce capabilities.[36]

[36] For a report that the United States will shortly have some such capability with the 647 satellite system, see *New York Times*, March 21, 1971. For an

Some observers have asserted that one consequence of area-ABM systems will be to decrease any incentive a power may have for firing several weapons to demonstrate "determination" or "intent," on the grounds that even a light area-ABM system could prevent such weapons from hitting a target.[37] The obverse would seem to be the more likely case. Since the purpose of firing for demonstration is to communicate willingness to risk war, in the hope that war can be avoided, it would seem to be a net benefit that such weapons would not necessarily result in actual damage to the enemy's people or forces. For in this case, the desired communication has been made with a minimum risk of exacerbating rather than easing the crisis. In short, the light area-ABM system, far from diminishing the attractiveness of demonstration firings, would seem almost to invite them.

IV

The prospective changes in the strategic environment outlined in the preceding section have the potential of affecting directly or indirectly every major military component in NATO's present security posture. To begin with, although the military security of Western Europe in the 1970s will continue to depend on the American commitment to respond to a Soviet attack with the use of strategic nuclear weapons if all other means fail, prospective developments in the strategic arms race will make it increasingly difficult for the United States to provide the kind of strategic forces and strategy to deliver on the commitment that will seem at one and the same time reliable to Western Europeans, tolerable to Russians, and acceptable to Americans.

In addition to the strain that developments in the strategic arms

---

argument on behalf of greater attention to limited counter-force doctrine, see Richard Rosecrance, "U.S. Strategy and the New Administration," in Paul Seabury and Aaron Wildavsky (eds.), *U.S. Foreign Policy: Perspectives and Proposals for the 1970s* (New York: McGraw-Hill Book Company, 1969), pp. 113–18.

[37] See Charles M. Herzfeld, "Missile Defense: Can It Work?," in Johan J. Holst and William Schneider, Jr. (eds.), *Why ABM?* (New York: Pergamon Press, 1969), p. 40.

race will place on the credibility of the American nuclear guarantee, the expenses of that race could also lead to significant changes in the other military components for the defense of Western Europe: the conventional and tactical nuclear forces of NATO. If the budget of the United States is subjected to the double pressure of upgraded domestic priorities and increased expenditures for strategic weapons, the United States might be led to reduce the size of its conventional forces in Western Europe. Should the Western European allies follow suit, NATO would have to place greater reliance on the use of tactical nuclear weapons. In the end NATO could find itself with a reduced capability for preventing violence from escalating rapidly to all-out war at the same time that a smaller American military presence may have increased doubts about the strength of the American political commitment to Western Europe, which is what serves to deter violence in the first place.

These are by no means improbable outcomes, as subsequent analysis will show, but they are not inevitable outcomes. Some could be modified by a SALT agreement, as the next section indicates. Others are contingent on the future actions of the Western Europeans and the Russians, discussed in Chapter Three, and all of these outcomes can be influenced by choices still open to the United States regarding its arms and arms control policies for strategic, conventional, and tactical nuclear forces, the subject of the last chapter of this book. But before sensible choices can be made, alternatives must be clear, and the purpose of this section is to indicate a course of events that unless checked by conscious choice could easily end up placing present European security arrangements under great strain.

A major opportunity for choice and an issue certain to cause debate will be the manner of financing the new expenditures for strategic forces that will occur in the absence of a comprehensive agreement from SALT. If the strategic arms race continues without check, the cost for strategic forces could easily rise by an additional $4–6 billion a year. Between inflation and the costs of supporting the force levels (strategic and general purpose) which the administration already plans to maintain over the next five years, there is no prospect that this additional $4–6 billion can be secured from the "savings" that will attend the termination of the war in Vietnam. The increased funds for strategic forces will have to come from either an increase in the size of the defense budget or a decrease in the size of the general purpose forces that the administration currently plans to maintain.[38]

The administration would find it politically very difficult, however, to finance major new expenditures for strategic weapons solely by increasing the size of the defense budget. Powerful elements in the public and in Congress are intent on making the end of the war in Vietnam an occasion for effecting major reductions in the *present* size of the defense budget. If the national mood continues to support a shift in priorities from foreign to domestic purposes and programs, the administration will be hard put to offset the political pressures on its present defense budget (which would rise in any event as a result of inflation and the costs of procurement programs now under way), much less to persuade Congress and the public to support a large increase in that budget.[39]

In the defense budget requested for fiscal year 1972, the cost (direct and indirect) of strategic forces is about $19.7 billion, which is about 25 percent of the total defense budget requested ($79.2 billion). If the cost of strategic forces rose by an additional $5 billion a year, neither their total cost ($25 billion a year) nor their share of the enlarged budget (about 30 percent) would be without precedent. In the FY 1964 defense budget, the share for strategic forces

[38] See Charles L. Schultze, Edward R. Fried, Alice M. Rivlin, and Nancy H. Teeters, *Setting National Priorities: The 1972 Budget* (Washington: The Brookings Institution, 1971) [hereafter cited as Brookings, *The 1972 Budget*], pp. 48, 49, 111; and statement by Secretary Laird, HCAS, *Hearings FY 1972 Budget*, pp. 2415, 2418. The budget figures cited in this section are for total obligational authority.

[39] On the expected rise in the cost of supporting present force levels, see Brookings, *The 1972 Budget*, pp. 38, 67. Illustrative of the order of cuts that have been suggested in the present budget, see the proposal for a $10 billion reduction advanced by Dr. Carl Kaysen, as reported in *New York Times*, February 13, 1971, and the nearly $16 billion reduction proposed by the staff of the Natinal Urban Coalition in Robert S. Benson and Harold Wolman (eds.), *Counterbudget: A Blueprint for Changing National Priorities, 1971–1976* (New York: Frederick A. Praeger, 1971) [hereafter cited as National Urban Coalition, *Counterbudget*], p. 273.

was about 33 percent, and their cost (measured in 1972 dollars) was about $25 billion. It is also the case that if the defense budget increased to $85 or even $90 billion, given a plausible rise in GNP, the nation would still be spending a smaller percentage of its GNP for defense than it did in FY 1964.[40]

But as the battle of the budget is joined, the advocates of increased spending for defense will find little political capital in the arithmetical precedents cited above. As in the past, the public and Congress will prove far more sensitive to changes in the absolute level of the defense budget than to changes in its percentage of the GNP or to the size of defense expenditures measured in the constant dollars of some bygone year. The Nixon administration is properly impressed by the fact that it has already accomplished a budgetary feat that has eluded every postwar administration in this century: it has kept the size of the FY 1972 budget (its first post-Vietnam budget), as measured in constant dollars, to about the size of the last prewar budget. But what is most likely to impress the general public is something else: the fact that in current dollars the administration is now proposing to spend for defense as much as the nation was spending during the peak year of the Vietnam war.[41]

A failure at SALT would result in a climate of opinion conducive to some rise in the defense budget, but the interest of the administration in keeping that budget as low as possible and the pressure from those who believe it is already much too high will

[40] In current dollars the cost for strategic forces in FY 1964 was $17.1 billion. This cost decreased to $14.2 billion in FY 1965 (amounting to 22 percent of the total defense budget) and from this low the cost for strategic forces has risen by 38 percent to the present $19.7 billion. These figures and those in the text are based on data in Brookings, *The 1972 Budget,* pp. 34–35, 39, 321; Charles L. Schultze, Edward K. Hamilton, and Allen Schick, *Setting National Priorities: The 1971 Budget* (Washington: The Brookings Institution, 1971) [hereafter cited as Brookings, *The 1971 Budget*], p. 50; and HCAS, *Hearings FY 1971 Budget,* p. 6906.

[41] For comparisons between the present and previous budgets (prewar and postwar), see HCAS, *Hearings FY 1972 Budget,* pp. 2417–18; and Warner R. Schilling, Paul Y. Hammond, and Glenn H. Snyder, *Strategy, Politics, and Defense Budgets* (New York: Columbia University Press, 1962), p. 30. The defense budget for FY 1969 was $79.4 billion; see HCAS, *Hearings FY 1971 Budget,* p. 6904.

combine to insure that a substantial amount of the new billions required for strategic forces will be secured by reducing the size (and hence the cost) of the nation's general purpose forces (divisions, tactical air groups, carrier task forces, etc.). In the FY 1972 budget, the cost of these forces is $51 billion, of which $25.4 billion are earmarked for NATO contingencies and $15.6 billion for non-Vietnam Asian contingencies.[42]

On the basis of these figures, it is evident that the cost of the additional $5 billion for strategic forces could be entirely covered by reducing the size of the general purpose forces presently budgeted for Asia. Given the present uncertainty about the course of events in Asia that will result from the American withdrawal from Vietnam, the administration might well hesitate to follow that withdrawal so quickly with what would amount to a substantial reduction from the size of its prewar military presence in Asia. Accordingly, if cuts have to be made in the size of the general purpose forces, the forces presently budgeted for NATO (which account for half the total cost of the general purpose forces) are unlikely to escape bearing some share of the reduction.[43]

[42] For these figures, see Brookings, *The 1972 Budget*, p. 55. The total cost of NATO-oriented general purpose forces in the budget request for FY 1971 was estimated to be $19.1 billion in Brookings, *The 1971 Budget*, p. 44. In contrast, the Department of Defense has given a $14 billion figure for the cost of NATO-oriented general purpose forces in three successive budgets: FY 1970, FY 1971, and FY 1972. Some of this disparity results from differences in accounting (e.g., the Department's figure does not include a share of research and development costs), but in addition the Department has stated that the Brookings 1971 study overestimated the total cost of the general purpose forces. In this event, the costs cited in this chapter for strategic forces are too low.

This chapter has used the figures from the Brookings studies because they provide the only available accounting of the total cost of strategic forces during recent years.

For the Department of Defense figures, see SCAS, *Hearings FY 1971 Budget*, p. 207; Senate Committee on Foreign Relations, Subcommittee on United States Agreements and Commitments Abroad, *Hearings, United States Security Agreements and Commitments Abroad*, 91st Cong., 2nd Sess. (reprinted 1971), pp. 2053–54; and HCAS, *Hearings FY 1972 Budget*, pp. 2597–98.

[43] Although one can anticipate a renewal of the 1948–49 Air Force–Army alliance for placing the burden of these cuts on the Navy's carrier forces, the politics of interservice rivalry will probably insure that the cuts are born by

This means that the pressure will mount once again to reduce the size of the American military presence in Western Europe. Although the cost of the forces actually in the European theater accounts for only about a third of the total cost of America's NATO-oriented general purpose forces, the forces in Europe have a high political visibility and have been the focus of most efforts to reduce the cost of America's NATO commitment, including Senator Mansfield's proposal to withdraw half of the 310,000 American servicemen in Europe by the end of 1971.[44]

President Nixon's affirmation that he will not reduce the present level of American forces without reciprocal action by the Soviet Union and the Senate's defeat of the Mansfield proposal notwithstanding, there may well be an increase in the strength of the complex of interests that have produced support for a reduction in the size of American forces in Europe: reduced fear of a Soviet attack, the belief that it is high time the Western Europeans took a larger part in providing for their defense, balance-of-payments pressures, the desire for reduced military commitments abroad in the aftermath of the disenchantment with Vietnam, and the belief that domestic problems deserve a higher priority than they have received in the past. To these considerations continued deployment of the MIRV-ABM technology would provide another: increased pressure on the defense budget as Americans labor under the unwelcome burden of increased expenditures for strategic arms.[45]

the arms of all three services. The political incentive for the Secretary to reduce the number of Army divisions will be strong, because this would justify proportionate reductions in the air support provided by both the Navy and the Air Force.

[44] The cost of the forces actually in Europe is estimated at $8 billion (of a total $25.4 billion for NATO-oriented forces) in Brookings, *The 1972 Budget*, p. 55. In contrast, the Department of Defense's figure is $3.2 billion of a total $14 billion. See HCAS, *Hearings FY 1972 Budget*, p. 2597. It would be possible to cut only the NATO-oriented forces stationed in the United States, but this alternative has received little attention, except in National Urban Coalition, *Counterbudget*, pp. 262–63, where the American-based forces are assigned a large share of the proposed total cut in the NATO-oriented forces.

[45] For the President's statement, see *The President: 1971 Foreign Policy Message*, p. 25. There would have been stronger support for the Mansfield amendment if Brezhnev had not made a statement raising hopes for a negotiated reduction that would include Soviet troops in Europe. Senator Mansfield

This last development might well provide both the rationale and the impetus for a major reduction in the size of the American forces in Europe. If so, there is little reason to believe that the Western Europeans would make up the difference by increasing the size of their own conventional forces. The Europeans have never taken the lead in arguing for increases in NATO's conventional capabilities, and while they will certainly view any reduction in the American contribution to that capability with concern, this concern will stem more from their worries about how the reduction will affect the strength of the American commitment to defend Western Europe than from any reservations about the military consequences of a reduced conventional-weapons capability in Western Europe.

The United States would no doubt endeavor to minimize these worries by prefacing any withdrawal of forces with careful consultation with the NATO allies and by accompanying that withdrawal with renewed and firm declarations regarding the continued American determination to defend Western Europe. However reassuring this consultation, it is not likely to lead the Western Europeans (who have budgetary pressures of their own) to decide to offset the American withdrawal. On the contrary, they are much more likely to make any American reduction the occasion for reducing the size of their own NATO forces.

The prospects for a large reduction in the conventional forces of NATO are not matched by the prospect of a proportionate reduction in those of the Warsaw Treaty Organization. Aside from the foreign-policy reasons why the Soviet Union might choose to play a waiting game and see what happens as NATO engages in a unilateral reduction of ground forces, Soviet force levels in Central Europe are likely to remain high as a result of policy considerations and needs that are not directly related to the size of NATO forces.

First, as the events in Czechoslovakia in the summer of 1968

---

is determined to reopen the issue and hopes to reduce the number of American divisions in Western Europe from the present four and one-third to one. See *New York Times*, May 16, 1971, and an Associated Press dispatch by Arthur Gavshon in *The Record* (Hackensack, N.J.), July 7, 1971.

once again demonstrated, the Soviet Union needs to maintain troops in Eastern Europe for reasons which have nothing to do with the problem of coping with the conventional forces of NATO. Moreover, unlike the United States in NATO, the Soviet Union cannot consider devolving onto its allies the direction and leadership of WTO forces nor face with equanimity the prospect of greater military dependence on the armed forces of those allies, including *its* Germans.

Second, although the Soviet Union will be subject to the same order of budgetary pressures from the new strategic weapons technology as here ascribed to the United States (and with a much smaller GNP), these pressures may not produce parallel changes in the two countries' conventional military postures. The technology of the 1970s will not come all at once, and while the Soviet Union and the United States seem certain to deploy MIRVs and (in the absence of an agreement to the contrary) ABMs, they will not do so at the same time. The American deployment of MIRVs is well under way. In contrast, the Soviet Union has yet to begin its test program. In the case of ABMs, here too Soviet technological capabilities appear to be less advanced than those of the United States. In short, there is a good prospect that the mid-1970s will find the Soviet Union confronting a rather impressive "warhead gap" that favors the United States.

In this event the Soviet Union might decide to maintain a superior European-theater capability until it had closed the strategic gap. Several students of Soviet policy have suggested that a major reason why the Soviet Union maintained a superior ground army facing Western Europe in the immediate postwar years was to hold Western Europe hostage for America's good behavior during the period of American nuclear monopoly. Whether this consideration actually contributed to the military posture of the Soviet Union in those years, it is certainly a tactic that may occur to the present Soviet leadership in the event of a MIRV-ABM gap. This tactic would require an occasional blunt reminder to the Western Europeans of their vulnerability to the Soviet MRBMs and IRBMs targeted against them, but it could also lead the Soviet Union to decide not to match any reduction in NATO's conventional forces with a significant withdrawal or demobilization of its own conventional forces in Central Europe.[46]

The deployment of the MIRV-ABM technology, then, may well be associated with the development of a marked asymmetry between the conventional forces of NATO and WTO. As a result, the NATO powers would be obliged to develop a strategy anticipating an earlier use of tactical nuclear weapons than that presently projected under the doctrine of flexible response, and the Americans would have to anticipate a somewhat earlier need to bring to bear the threat of the use of American strategic nuclear forces.

In their general outline these developments might not seem unlike those that followed the Korean War: a decreasing American defense budget that led to an increase in reliance on nuclear weapons for the defense of Western Europe (in the form of the doctrine of massive retaliation for the deterrent use of strategic nuclear forces and of the introduction of tactical nuclear weapons for battlefield defense and interdiction). In their general form neither of these developments would appear to pose any serious problems for the relations between the United States and its NATO allies. The Western Europeans have always wanted deterrence, not defense, whether defense meant their having to bear a larger share of the costs of large ground forces for a possible war in Europe or their having to anticipate the destruction that the actual employment of those forces might entail for Western Europe. They have been quite willing to rely on the deterrent effect of the threat to use nuclear weapons, whether strategic or tactical.

But the general parallel with the development of policy immediately after the Korean war is deceptive. As previously noted, the advent of warhead plenty, together with ABM defenses and improved intelligence systems, is likely to stimulate an interest in a doctrine of limited strategic war, with an accent on counterforce exchanges designed to demonstrate intentions rather than to destroy capabilities. As a result, while a reduction in conventional

---

[46] For possible earlier use by the Soviet Union of a "hostage" strategy and a review of current policy considerations affecting the size of Soviet forces in Eastern Europe, see Thomas W. Wolfe, *Soviet Power and Europe: 1945–1970*, pp. 33–34, 460–64.

forces in Europe may place renewed emphasis in NATO strategy on the United States' commitment to use its strategic forces, the doctrine that is likely to guide those forces is going to seem far more similar to that advanced by Robert McNamara in 1962 than it is to that enunciated by John Foster Dulles in 1954. Moreover, unlike the case in 1962, when the strategic inferiority of the Soviet Union gave it little interest in city-avoidance strategy, once the Soviet Union has deployed its own version of an ABM system and successfully MIRVed its own missile forces, it will be similarly in a position to anticipate a series of counterforce exchanges that would not threaten to exhaust the warheads necessary to achieve "assured destruction" of the United States.

Seen in these terms, the development of American strategic doctrine would pose serious problems for the Western Europeans. Their reaction to the 1962 city-avoidance strategy was by no means favorable, and there is no evident reason why they should think any better of it in the 1970s. The American interest in terminating a conflict in Europe in some manner that does not result in the total devastation of American society is strong and sensible. But the Western Europeans want the Soviet Union to be deterred by the threat of countercity war, and they will be understandably fearful of any American strategy that seems to hold open to the Soviet Union the prospect that its cities will not be hit soon and hard. For in their view this would encourage the Soviet Union to take risks in Europe that it would otherwise not consider and would invite consequences for NATO that could fall most disproportionately on Western Europe.

The disputes that may occur over the development of American strategic doctrine in the 1970s will be further complicated by disputes that will attend the development of doctrine for the use of tactical nuclear weapons. In the 1960s, NATO's doctrine for tactical nuclear war, at least as seen in the public record, appeared to be the orphan child of military planning. The weapons were there, indeed the number of warheads deployed in Europe almost doubled, but strategy seemed intent on putting them out of mind, if not out of sight.

Strategy for the use of tactical nuclear weapons is unlikely to remain in political limbo in the 1970s, especially if the NATO powers should decrease the size of their conventional forces. The development of mutually satisfactory doctrine may be complicated, however, by a slight shading in the perspectives with which the allies will approach the issues involved. By Americans tactical nuclear weapons are viewed as an adjunct to the defense of Western Europe, and their use is seen as a way of putting off and hopefully forestalling the employment of strategic nuclear weapons. But by Western Europeans, who have no interest in inhabiting a nuclear battlefield, tactical nuclear weapons are seen as an adjunct to deterrence, and the early use of such weapons against the Soviet Union is seen as a way of insuring escalation to the use of strategic weapons and thereby preventing war in the first place.[47]

As in the case of strategic weapons, it will not be easy for the NATO powers to find a doctrine that will provide a common focus for these divergent perspectives. Plans and dispositions that may lead to a large-scale and uncontrolled use of tactical nuclear weapons or to their early use on Soviet territory could easily negate any possibility for terminating hostilities without the all-out use of strategic nuclear forces. On the other hand, a strategy for a very limited and highly controlled use of tactical nuclear weapons, coupled with a comparable doctrine for the use of strategic nuclear weapons, especially if added to an asymmetry in conventional forces in Europe, could combine to undermine any conviction among the Western Europeans that NATO could provide effectively for either defense or deterrence.

Politically, then, the United States and the Western Europeans could end up with the worst of both the worlds of John Foster Dulles and Robert McNamara. The Americans (given reduced NATO conventional forces and plans for an earlier use of tactical nuclear weapons) would have all of their "1954 worries" about the NATO commitment moving them too rapidly toward World War III, and the Europeans (given an American and Soviet interest in

---

[47] For an illuminating insight into European thinking on doctrine for tactical nuclear weapons, see Gen. Pasti Nino (former Deputy for Nuclear Affairs to the Supreme Allied Commander Europe), "NATO's Defense Strategy," *Orbis*, Spring 1969, pp. 111–32.

limited strategic war) would have all of their "1962 worries" about being the subject of Soviet-American strategic bargaining while they were being run over and blown up by the Red Army.

Actually, the strain on the alliance could be greater than these historical parallels suggest. For in the 1970s the American worry about Western Europe's increased dependence on the threat of strategic nuclear war may be heightened by the recognition that the new weapons technology will provide a greater strain toward preemptive action than did the weapons technology of the 1950s. And Western Europeans' confidence in American strategic doctrine will be ebbing in a time when in contrast to the early 1960s the Soviet Union will appear both more powerful and less threatening.

In summary, the new strategic environment could set in motion a train of events and choices that would lead to a significant change from present European security arrangements. Militarily, there would be little left of NATO but an American nuclear shelter, and the Western Europeans would be provided with a security "free ride." But it might prove neither a smooth nor a long ride. The Americans could come increasingly to resent the burden of the carrying and the West Europeans to question the quality of the shelter, and as Chapters Four and Five explain in detail, a free-ride Western Europe arrangement could turn out to be only a transition to other, more radical departures from present European security arrangements.

V

An answer to the question of how the prospect just described would be changed by a SALT agreement must distinguish not only between the two agreements that might emerge from SALT but also between the effects of these agreements on the stability of the strategic balance and their effects on the stability of present European security arrangements, for an agreement on the American proposal is more likely to improve the stability of the first than that of the second, and an agreement on the Russian proposal may not improve the stability of either.

A Soviet-American agreement to ban or limit ABMs would, of

course, deprive the superpowers of the means for an active defense of their land-based missiles and bombers against a first strike and their cities against a second strike. It is this second feature of the agreement that would improve the stability of the strategic balance, for the superpowers would no longer have to worry about the possibility that ABMs might be built to defend cities and thereby downgrade the effectiveness of their second-strike capabilities. In contrast to a world which included ABMs, the strategic balance would be more certain, and in the absence of area or city defenses the superpowers might also be somewhat less attracted to limited strategic war doctrine.

The difficulty with a SALT agreement that covers only ABMs, which is essentially the Soviet proposal, is that it leaves the superpowers to confront the threat which MIRV will bring to their ICBMs while depriving them of what may be the least provocative way they have of meeting that threat. As explained in Section II, of the nine ways the superpowers can meet the MIRV threat, the defend choice would disturb the strategic balance least, provided (and it is a critical provision) each superpower could and would deploy its ABMs for ICBM defense in such a manner that the other could not mistake the deployment for a city-defense system.

The full effect on the strategic balance of a SALT agreement limited to ABMs will turn, therefore, on the kind of choices the superpowers then make to meet the MIRV threat. If one or both superpowers should place their land-based missiles on a launch-on-warning status, the increased possibility of war by computer or radar failure will lead many to wonder if the SALT agreement will not have resulted in a net loss for arms control. Much the same judgment would attend a future in which the superpowers engaged in the multiplication of their ICBMs. On the other hand, if the superpowers decide to invest in whole new weapons systems, whether sea- or land-based, the SALT agreement could lead, paradoxically, to a net increase in expenditures for strategic weapons.

So far as European security arrangements are concerned, a SALT agreement limited to ABMs would probably result in much the same kind of budgetary pressure on American conventional forces for NATO as was projected for the contingency of no agreement on strategic arms. In the absence of the defense option, the United States would probably decide to meet the problem of Minuteman vulnerability with an earlier commitment to ULMS than would otherwise have been the case and perhaps with a new strategic bomber as well. Since Safeguard was intended to provide also for bomber defense against SLBMs, new programs for bomber basing and alert would be considered. Finally, there would be strong pressure to deploy the shelter-based Minuteman, for, as previously noted, so long as the Soviet Union maintains ICBMs, the United States will be reluctant to abandon its own. Whatever the mix finally chosen among these programs, their total cost could easily exceed the dollars saved by scrapping Safeguard and preventing the construction of the Hardsite system.[48]

The consequences that would follow from a SALT agreement along the lines of the initial American proposal are more complex. In addition to limiting ABMs, the American proposal would fix a ceiling on the total number of delivery vehicles (ICBMs, SLBMs, and long-range bombers) that each side could maintain, with each side free to determine on its own mix within this total number, subject to the condition that neither would deploy more than a given number (reported to be 300) of the SS-9 type of missiles. Finally, the United States has also proposed a ban on land-mobile ICBMs.[49]

The most important effect of a Soviet-American agreement to maintain the same number of delivery vehicles would be political. The agreement would affirm the interest of the superpowers in moderating their strategic competition, and it would symbolize to the Russians (and the Western Europeans) the willingness of the United States to accept strategic equality with the Soviet Union. The existence of the ceiling would also have significant military effects. It would restrict the range of choice open to the superpowers to meet the MIRV threat to their ICBMs, and it would bring a halt to the quantitative side of the strategic arms race. The size of the

[48] See fn. 24, and *New York Times*, December 7, 1970.
[49] Institute for Strategic Studies, *Strategic Survey 1970* (London: Institute for Strategic Studies, 1971), p. 12; and *New York Times*, December 24, 1970 and January 17, 1971.

ceiling (some 1900 vehicles) would require the United States to reduce its present number of delivery vehicles by some 320, which
could be done by retiring the requisite number of B-52 bombers,
most of which were due to be phased out of service in any event.
The ceiling would present the Soviet Union with a more difficult
choice, for it would be unable to increase its number of Polaris-
type submarines up to the American total without making corresponding reductions in its presently superior number of ICBMs.[50]

For the immediate strategic balance, however, the most significant feature of the American proposal is the provision to limit the
number of SS-9 missiles. The effect of this limit could be to postpone until the 1980s the kind of MIRV threat the United States has
heretofore been afraid could materialize in the mid-1970s. Against
a Soviet SS-9 force limited to 300 missiles (and given the same
order of accuracy and reliability previously expected for the
MIRVed warheads of these missiles in the mid-1970s), a 1000-silo
intermediate hardening program could insure the survival of some
23 percent of the Minuteman force. This would leave the United
States with a still-impressive land-based deterrent. The number of
remaining warheads could even be increased if the United States
MIRVed its entire Minuteman force (which would not be prohib-
ited by the terms of the agreement), and the number of surviving
Minutemen could be increased if the negotiated ABM limitation
permitted the United States to retain limited defenses around one
or more Minuteman fields in exchange for a limited Soviet deployment around Moscow.[51]

[50] Institute for Strategic Studies, *The Military Balance 1970–1971*, p. 87,
states that although some 60 percent of American missile-firing submarines can
be kept on station, logistical and geographic factors would permit the Soviet
Union to maintain only 40 percent of its submarines on station. In this event
numerical equality in submarines would provide for something less than strategic equality. However, this is only one among many significant differences
(e.g., in accuracy, payload, range) in the strategic missile forces of the superpowers that makes the ceiling of greater symbolic than military significance.

[51] For indications that the United States plans to upgrade the hardness of
all 1000 Minuteman silos, see HCAS, *Hearings FY 1972 Budget*, pp. 2919–20,
3051. The estimate of 23 percent assumes that the silos will be able to withstand 900 psi and that the SS-9s will carry six 2MT warheads with the same
retargeting and other capabilities previously expected (see fn. 5). A three 5MT
configuration would result in about 40 percent survival and an 18 200KT configuration in about 35 percent survival.

But the American proposal provides no better insurance for the long-run survival of Minuteman than it does for the Soviet ICBMs. In time, the security of both forces will be undermined by improvements in the accuracy and reliability of their MIRVed missiles. Thus, the protection afforded by the new American hardening program and the SS-9 limitation would be lost as soon as the accuracy of the SS-9 force dropped from the presently projected 1500-foot CEP to a CEP of about 1000 feet, and the same result would obtain if the Soviet Union made major improvements in the accuracy of its SS-11 ICBMs.

The terms of the American proposal, however, would rule out a number of the ways in which the superpowers might respond to the forthcoming vulnerability of their ICBMs (aside from eliminating the option of defense). Hiding missiles or building fake silos would be viewed by the other side as permitting a potential violation of the agreement to limit the total number of delivery vehicles. The agreement would also effectively prevent the superpowers from employing the multiplication option: given the prospective vulnerability of fixed-site ICBMs, neither side would choose to increase the number of such missiles in its total delivery force. Two other options—doing nothing and superhardening—although not prevented by the terms of the agreement, can also be ruled out for the reasons discussed in Section II.

The United States and the Soviet Union would have to choose, then, among the remaining three alternatives: placing their ICBMs on a launch-on-warning status; writing off their land-based missiles over time and adding instead to the quality and quantity of their bombers and submarine-launched missiles; replacing their fixed-site ICBMs with land-mobile ICBMs. If the Soviet Union agreed to a ban on mobile ICBMs, even this last alternative would not be available. The terms of the agreement would appear, in any event, to rule out the deployment of the American shelter-based Minuteman, because a mobile system of this order could also be viewed as a "faking" or "hiding" alternative and a potential violation of the ceiling on the total number of delivery vehicles.

In summary, although a SALT agreement based on the American proposal provides no more satisfactory long-run answer to the MIRV threat than would an agreement based on the Soviet proposal, there are important differences between the two in terms of their effect on the strategic balance. First, under the American proposal, the MIRV threat would be slower to materialize. The Soviet threat to American ICBMs would have to wait on further improvements in missile accuracy, a situation which already obtains in the case of the American threat to Soviet ICBMs. Second, an agreement to the American proposal would permit both sides to plan to meet the MIRV threat to ICBMs in the knowledge that each would refrain from certain alternatives (multiplying, hiding, faking, and moving) and that whatever else happened each side's total number of delivery vehicles would remain constant. This situation would enable each to rule out at least some greater-than-expected threats for planning purposes. Accordingly, the stability of the strategic balance would be significantly improved over that resulting from a SALT agreement limited only to ABMs.

The two agreements also differ in their potential effect on European security arrangements. In contrast to an agreement limited to ABMs or no agreement at all, the budgetary pressure to reduce American conventional forces for NATO would probably be less in the event of a SALT agreement based on the American proposal. The cost of strategic forces will not go down in the event of such an agreement, but the cost is unlikely to increase quite so much as it would in the other two cases. It would be politically infeasible for the United States government to follow a Soviet agreement to its SALT proposal by a large increase in its budget for strategic arms. The need for MIRV-offsetting programs will not be removed by the agreement, but the climate of détente that would attend the agreement, together with the terms of the agreement itself, would lead to a lower GET than would otherwise be the case and hence to a smaller rise in the cost of strategic forces.

Reduced pressure on the budget would not cancel out all the other interests that have pressed for a reduction in the size of the American military presence in Europe, and the détente that would follow the SALT agreement would no doubt further undermine the American sense of the need to maintain those forces at their present size. But a SALT agreement would also raise hopes that a formal agreement could be reached to reduce NATO-WTO force levels, and the political effect of these hopes would be to encourage the NATO powers not to engage in unilateral force reductions until they had explored the possibility of formal bilateral reductions.

An agreement to the American SALT proposal would, then, delay but not necessarily prevent movement toward the nuclear-sheltered Western Europe that was projected in the case of no agreement at all or one limited to ABMs. The point is critical, for a nuclear-sheltered Europe would be an even less stable security arrangement in the event of an agreement to the American proposal. Since such an agreement would provide the Soviet Union with politically recognized parity, it would stimulate and renew Western European reservations about the quality of the American nuclear guarantee.

The reliability of this commitment has, of course, been questioned before and would be reviewed in any event as a result of recent Soviet strides in the arms race, since the United States has not had for some years sufficient counterforce superiority to deprive the Soviet Union of a devastating second-strike capability. Nonetheless, in the absence of a SALT agreement a continued arms race might serve to maintain some belief in American strategic superiority, especially during the period when the United States would lead in the deployment of MIRVs and ABMs. But the signing of a formal agreement with the Soviet Union that would provide a codification of parity would symbolize a revolutionary change in the perceived strategic balance, and the agreement would certainly serve as a catalyst for serious debate in Western Europe about the reliability of the American nuclear guarantee.[52]

[52] The SALT agreements signed in May 1972 are a variation on the proposals discussed above, but they will have substantially the same military, political, and budgetary effects.

The ABM treaty, which limits the superpowers to 100 interceptors at each of two sites (the national capital and one ICBM field), deprives the superpowers of the means for an effective active defense against a missile attack directed at their ICBM sites, bomber bases, or cities. Since the cost to the United States of deploying the permitted two-site system will be about the same as the cost of building the previously authorized Safeguard defense for four ICBM fields and the treaty will permit continued research and development for ABM defense (and the construction of the radars for a Hardsite de-

VI

In the 1970s, with or without SALT agreements, changes in military technology and strategy promise to produce much the same effects as they have in the past: they will strain the Soviet-American balance of terror and provide the opportunity for the United States and its European allies to debate and divide over the meaning of those changes for NATO policy. But in the 1970s the strategic dilemma of the United States—to bridge between its balance-of-terror policies and its balance-of-power policies—will be more acute, for the United States will confront for the first time the problems of making its commitment to Europe credible in the face

---

fense at the ICBM field), the treaty is unlikely to lead to any significant reduction in the American defense budget. The treaty, however, will prevent the increase in that budget which would have followed from the deployment of the full 12-site Safeguard program or of a city-defense ABM system.

There are several differences between the terms of the Interim Agreement on offensive weapons and the terms of the original American proposal for these weapons: a common ceiling of 1900 delivery vehicles—ICBMs, SLBMs, and strategic bombers—with each side free to vary the mix among these three kinds of vehicles, provided the total number of SS-9-type ICBMs did not exceed 300.

The 1900 ceiling would have permitted the United States to maintain its 1000-Minuteman ICBM force, its 656 SLBMs, and (if the 54 older Titan II ICBMs were dismantled) a 244 bomber force, about the size of the planned B-1 purchase. The 1900 ceiling would have required the Soviet Union (assuming it continued to maintain 140 strategic bombers) to reduce its number of ICBMs (about 1527 deployed in May 1972) to a number close to the size of the American force (1104), if it desired to increase its number of SLBMs (about 430 deployed in May 1972) to match the American total of 656.

The Interim Agreement, in contrast, does not cover strategic bombers at all, and in the case of ICBMs and SLBMs permits the two powers to maintain all the launchers they had built or building in May 1972. As a result, the Soviet Union is permitted 2358 missile launchers (1618 ICBM launchers and 740 SLBM launchers), while the United States is limited to 1710 missile launchers (1054 ICBMs and 656 SLBMs). The terms of the Agreement, however, are designed to limit the Soviet Union to no more than 313 SS-9-type ICBM launchers.

If the numbers of strategic bombers maintained by the two powers in May 1972 are added to these potential missile numbers, the total number of delivery vehicles is more nearly equal (about 2498 for the Soviet Union and 2237 for the United States), but this "de facto" ceiling is far higher than the 1900 figure proposed by the United States, and it is not a true ceiling. There is

of Soviet strategic power equivalent to its own. Similarly, the next round of Western European reservations and resentments over American policy will occur in a strategic environment in which the American nuclear guarantee may seem less reliable and the Soviet Union both more powerful and less hostile.

These new circumstances will require both the United States and the Western Europeans to reexamine the nature of the Soviet threat to Western Europe and its relation to American strategic deterrence. Equally critical for future European security arrangements and for arms control will be the choices that the NATO powers make regarding tactical nuclear weapons policy and the

---

nothing in the Agreement to prevent the United States from adding bombers to close the numerical gap (or the Soviet Union from adding bombers to keep it open). The Interim Agreement does not permit varying the mix between bombers and missiles. The Agreement does permit some substitution of SLBMs for ICBMs, although the Soviet Union is permitted the greater number of conversions. The United States can convert a maximum of 54 ICBM launchers to SLBM launchers, and the Soviet Union a maximum of 210.

The Interim Agreement, by assigning the Soviet Union the superior number of missile launchers, promises to accent the advent of strategic parity (and the political and military issues associated with this event) even more than would have an agreement to the original American proposal. The Interim Agreement is also likely to produce greater pressure for increased expenditures on strategic weapons than would have the original proposal. The United States is already striving to offset the quantitative superiority of the Soviet Union by additional expenditures to improve the qualitative performance of its offensive systems, and the Soviet Union will no doubt endeavor to improve the quality of its systems in order to capitalize on its quantitative edge.

The ABM treaty, by removing the defense option, will require the superpowers to seek other ways to meet the MIRV threat to their ICBMs. The provisions of the Interim Agreement prohibit the options of multiplying, faking, hiding, or superhardening ICBMs. If the United States stands by or succeeds in persuading the Soviet Union to accept its unilateral declaration that the deployment of land-mobile ICBMs would be inconsistent with the objectives of the agreement, the superpowers will also be deprived of this option.

In the long run (unless the superpowers are able to negotiate a ban or limit on MIRV deployment or are willing to reopen one or another of the options foreclosed by SALT Phase I), the superpowers will be obliged to choose among the remaining alternatives: doing nothing, abandoning ICBMs, or preparing to launch them on warning. In the short run, however, the superpowers are likely to continue to spend money to prolong the second-strike capability of their ICBMs by intermediate hardening and by adding to the number of warheads on their ICBMs.

manner in which they coordinate strategy for the use of these weapons with that for the use of strategic weapons. Finally and perhaps of the greatest political consequence will be the effect of the new strategic environment on the decisions reached regarding the size of NATO's conventional forces and most particularly the size of the American military presence in Western Europe.

The final chapter of this book outlines perspectives and pre-scribes choices on all of these issues. The purpose of this chapter has been to demonstrate the potential of the new strategic environ-ment for producing choices that could result in significant changes in present European security arrangements. A clear prospect is that Western Europeans may become even more dependent on American nuclear weapons for their security. The impetus in this direction would be provided by the American preoccupation with the strategic arms race, the consequent withdrawal of a large num-ber of American troops from Europe, and a subsequent reduction in conventional forces by the Western European powers. Much the same result could follow from a SALT agreement if the ensuing sense of détente should lead the NATO powers to reduce their conventional forces without compensating demobilization by the Soviet Union.

Beyond this prospect there are others. The Western Europeans are likely to find themselves increasingly at odds with the United States over what doctrine will govern the use of strategic and tacti-cal weapons, with the consequence that American nuclear power may appear progressively less relevant to the political needs and interests of the Europeans. If relations with the Soviet Union con-tinue to lead the Western Europeans to believe there is little pros-pect of a direct attack from that country and if at the same time the Western Europeans should become increasingly worried about the possibility of American foreign policy involving them in a war arising from non-European issues, then the prospective develop-ments in military strategy and technology here described could help move Western Europe toward a more autonomous and inde-pendent security posture.

The key impetus for movement in this direction, however, is more likely to come from political than from military developments. Although one might expect the Western Europeans to become increasingly worried about the possibility that instabilities in the Soviet-American balance of terror might involve them in war, especially in the MIRV-ABM world, most Europeans appear to be considerably less worried by such a prospect than are many Americans. Europeans tend to view the refined and imaginative instability scenarios of American strategists as a rather special, esoteric, intellectual endeavor that has little political relevance to the real world.

In contrast to what will probably be a relative lack of concern over the instability of the balance of terror, the Western Europeans can be expected to show considerable interest in the question of whether American foreign policies in other parts of the world might carry with them the consequence of involving NATO in a war with the Soviet Union. If after the end of the Vietnam war the United States is seized by a desire for withdrawal from overseas commitments and interventions, the Western Europeans will have relatively little cause for worry. But such possibilities in the 1970s as a Soviet-American confrontation in the Middle East or a Soviet-Chinese rapprochement followed by a Chinese-American crisis could significantly affect Western Europeans' expectations and their interest in a more independent security posture.

This last prospect illustrates the point made at the beginning of the chapter: security arrangements are the product of the political goals and expectations of nations as well as of their military capabilities. The military developments discussed in this chapter clearly promise to strain present European security arrangements, but whether the Western Europeans in the 1970s take a security free ride, move toward a more independent security posture, or end up in some other or the same old security arrangement will also depend on the character of the changes and continuities in the economic and political environment. And it is with prospective trends and developments in this environment that the next chapter is concerned.

/ Chapter Three

the changing economic
and political environment

For those who lived through the late 1960s, the forecasting of political and security developments will always be an enterprise approached with caution and hedged with myriad disclaimers. The specific limits of prediction were all too clearly evident in those remarkable twelve months beginning in March 1968 which saw—among other things—the abrupt departure from public life of both Lyndon Johnson and Charles de Gaulle, the decisive end to Czechoslovak hopes for peaceful evolution toward a less authoritarian system, and the beginning of the protracted end of the Vietnam war under a man once viewed as the archetypal Cold Warrior. When one subsequently adds the Nixon visit to China, the Korean reconcilation attempts (however limited), and the economic side effects of the SALT Phase I agreements, the perils of detailed forecasting even within ranges of probable occurrence and broad confidence estimates should be so patent as to dissuade all but the most intrepid analysts.

Yet if the decade is taken as the unit of analysis, some of these hazards seem to diminish. By the middle 1960s, for example, one could have forecast with considerable confidence the passing of de Gaulle, the Vietnam war, and the Sino-American variant of the

Cold War within the next decade—and indeed some of the better futurologists did so. As for the Soviet military intervention in Czechoslovakia, the particular event may have been unpredictable, but so was the emergence of Dubček, which gave rise to it. In a longer perspective, the "surprising" Soviet intervention in Czechoslovakia was just one more demonstration of the Soviet Union's long-run determination to exercise hegemony over Eastern Europe.

On the assumption, then, that long-run trends can be discerned when the content of next week's headlines cannot, this chapter describes some major economic and political developments that can be expected to affect European security arrangements during the 1970s.

I

The most useful questions that can be asked about the effect of economic developments on European security arrangements in the next decade are the following: (1) Is there any likelihood that future economic developments in Western or Eastern Europe or in the United States or in the Soviet Union will by themselves compel the abandonment of existing security arrangements? (2) Does Western Europe possess or can it develop over the next ten years the economic and technological basis for producing deterrence and defense capabilities that would permit it to provide for its own security? (3) Will the progressive economic integration now under way in Western Europe exert a significant push toward military and political unification? (4) Are there at work in Western and Eastern Europe powerful forces such as the expansion of inter-regional trade which could propel the two regions toward an all-European community characterized by peaceful relations among members and by controlled and perhaps reduced military capabilities? [1]

The answer to the first question is an unqualified no. The leading European members of the North Atlantic alliance should be

[1] This analysis is heavily indebted to Klaus Knorr, "Economic Factors in Future Arrangements for European Security" in the companion volume *European Security and the Atlantic System* (New York: Columbia University Press, 1973).

able to maintain their present level of military effort (4 to 5 percent of gross national product) even if, as is quite possible, the rate of growth in their GNPs falls off. Many poorer countries, some of them much poorer, have been spending a higher proportion of their GNPs for defense.[2] In fact, with slower growth and hence probably reduced inflationary pressure, less rapidly rising prices would make it politically easier for governments to secure a given amount of defense goods. And in the very unlikely event that national incomes should decline sharply, governments would not be disposed in an era dominated by Keynesian concepts to cut any public expenditures, including defense outlays.

Similarly, the American economy can confidently be expected to bear defense outlays sufficient for the United States to maintain its present strategic deterrence posture vis-à-vis the Soviet Union. Moreover, pressure on the United States' balance of payments will not by itself force that country to cut its military forces in Europe as long as West German offset transactions continue to cover the bulk of foreign-exchange outlays incurred by the American military presence in Germany and other military outlays for Europe remain at their present modest levels.[3] Achieving a decisive strategic superiority over the Soviet Union, however, would probably require considerably increased defense outlays, plus superb military management, and possibly also scientific-technological luck. How large a total outlay the economy could bear would probably never be discovered, because political and social considerations would set ceilings long before economic limitations came into effect.

Finally, the growth rate of the Soviet GNP is such (higher than

[2] See, for example, ACDA's estimate that of the twenty-six states devoting 5 percent or more of their GNP to military expenditures fifteen have *per capita* income levels below that generally accepted as the threshold for economic "takeoff," namely, $300 per year. U.S. Arms Control and Disarmament Agency, *World Military Expenditures, 1969*, p. 5.

[3] In a January, 1970 speech to the Chicago Council on Foreign Relations (reprinted in *Survival*, March, 1970), the then Undersecretary of State, Elliot Richardson, said $1.5 billion annually was the total "drain" involved in military deployment. In recent years Bonn alone has made annual offset purchases —armaments, short- and long-term securities, gold-stock arrangements and the like—amounting to $500 million. See also Annette Baker Fox's findings in "Domestic Pressures in North America to Withdraw Forces from Europe," *European Security and the Atlantic System*.

that of the United States or Western Europe) that Soviet governments will be able to maintain current military outlays without difficulty and while permitting, if they wish, a steady and perceptible expansion of private consumption. Whether the Soviet economy could keep pace with a new American effort to achieve a decisive military superiority or would have the capability to make such an effort itself is again a question more for political than economic analysis. As in the American case political limits would become operative long before economic restraints.

With regard to the second question, the economic potential of Western European countries to provide capabilities for their own security, it should be noted that they have a conventional-weapons potential right now. Britain and the European Economic Community countries have a combined GNP substantially greater than that of the Soviet Union. If they had been spending for defense the same proportion of GNP that the United States has been spending and had been receiving contributions from the other Western European countries, they would certainly have had sufficient funds to provide a defense adequate to protect Western Europe.

Available funds are only part of the problem; the real capacity or the means of creating it has to exist, too. In one of the most basic resources, people, the major Western European countries slightly outnumber the Soviet Union. With respect to capacity to provide conventional military supplies and equipment, the major Western European countries exceed the Soviet Union in three measures indicative of such a capacity: crude steel production, motor vehicle production, and electricity output. It is true that Western Europe is less self-sufficient in basic resources, especially energy sources such as oil, than is the Soviet Union and can be expected to become increasingly dependent on imports. But the Western European governments' military buildup would be taking place in time of peace, when foreign trade is uninterrupted, and even in the case of modest attacks the Atlantic approaches to Europe presumably would remain open.

The situation ten years from now, however, depends on relative growth rates during the intervening period. It is expected that the Western European countries will maintain their slight lead in population, but that their economies will grow less than will the Soviet economy, with the result that by 1978 their combined GNP will probably be about 10 percent less than that of the Soviet Union. This differential or even a considerably larger one would not, of course, doom the Western Europeans' abilities to provide their own defense, especially since their defense efforts would act as a major stimulus to economic growth, and some of the Soviet military resources would have to be used outside Europe, notably in the Far East.

But to be fully security-independent, Western Europe would have to supply its own means for strategic nuclear deterrence. Unlike its situation with regard to conventional-weapons production, it presently lacks such a capability, with its requirements for computer, aerospace, and large-scale nuclear weapons industries. Britain and France have a sizable but nevertheless inadequate capacity for such products. Expansion of these industries would require a large and steady demand, a large scale of production, and time. Even then the initial effort would be difficult because of shortages of knowledge and skills, although imports of components could partially compensate for the shortages and the very strong balance-of-payments position of the region as a whole would permit such imports.

The real problem lies in the size of the market and scale of production. To yield unit costs low enough to be politically acceptable, production of strategic-deterrence weapons would have to be undertaken on a region-wide basis; separate national markets and production would be proscribed. The consolidation of markets and production efforts in Western Europe would tend to require other changes in the military picture: more consolidation of research and development efforts, greater uniformities in training and matériel, better proportioning of forces, and establishment of a unified command structure.

Thus the necessary conditions for obtaining the capacity to provide independently for strategic nuclear deterrence would seem to require a close defensive alliance among the EEC countries and Britain, plus a unitary market for defense products. Working against such an alliance and market are the rigidities and inertia of nationally separate military services and government ministries, the hesitation of leaders to give up actual or potential productive capacity to another country, and difficulties in securing agreement on how the financial costs and benefits of the new capability are to be distributed. Integration of military services and command structures would require integration of all foreign policies that are sensitive to the presence of military power. In short, it seems fair to say that Western Europe could provide its own strategic deterrence and thus gain full security independence only if it were far along the way toward a federal political structure. Since it would take years of negotiations and implementation to produce the federal structure after the desire for it was manifested, and further years to develop the industries necessary for a strategic nuclear deterrence capability, it is virtually certain that Western Europe could not be ready by 1980 to provide its own defense.

The answer to the third question, whether the economic integration now under way in Western Europe can be expected to exert a significant push toward military and political unification, is no. On the contrary, the economic impulses behind the movement toward economic integration have been losing force, and unless a substantial push is given it by military and political integration, not much further economic integration is likely to occur.

The EEC has successfully established a *customs* union. The next step would be *economic* union, which requires common fiscal and monetary systems, common trade, agricultural, transport, industrial, and labor policies and practices. But trying to achieve the necessary degree of uniformity runs up against basic differences between countries in political and social institutions and patterns of behavior. Despite the high-sounding resolve of meetings like the October 1972 EEC summit, moves toward a monetary union quickly run up against the strength of the West German mark vis-à-vis the French franc, which reflects differing monetary policies, trade union structures, savings practices, and export patterns. Adoption of common policies can cause social upheaval and consequent difficulties for political leaders, as with the recent proposal to rationalize agricultural production within the EEC, which would retire about 10 million acres and a large number of farmers. Moreover, the integration of economic policies requires adopting a common course of action on problems involving inflation, employment, and redistributive finance; such a common course could scarcely be achieved through the mechanism of periodic meetings of officials from each country. A supranational organization would have to exist.

The Western European countries might overcome the political and social barriers to economic union if the economic motivation were strong enough, i.e., if the alternative to economic union were stagnation, depression, and unemployment. But a Western Europe with a free-trade area secured by its customs union can be prosperous without economic union. It might be more prosperous with economic union (although some areas would of course be less prosperous), and indeed some slow progress toward a partial economic union may be made during the 1970s, mainly through the harmonizing of various countries' national economic policies. But substantial movements toward economic union can come only from political impetuses, such as a desire to bolster a move toward political integration with accompanying economic integration. And although the effect of Britain's EEC membership will be to expand the ties that bind all of Western Europe through the closer association of all former European Free Trade Area states with the EEC, the absorption of so large a trading country (as well as two smaller units) will necessitate major readjustments in all areas of community activity and will surely deflect much of the EEC's integrating energies through the mid-1970s.

To answer the fourth question, whether an expansion of trade and other economic cooperation between the countries of Western and Eastern Europe could lead to creation of a cooperative and peaceful all-European security community, one must ask first whether there is likely to be an expansion of trade between the two regions. Although it has been rising strongly over the past decade, the present volume of trade between the two areas is still extremely small, considering the relatively high industrialization of both areas. In 1967 only 6.5 percent of EEC imports were from, and 6.7 percent of EEC exports were to, Warsaw Treaty Organization countries.[4] The low level of trade can be explained by the

[4] West Germany's much discussed "Eastern trade offensive" from 1963 to 1967 resulted in an export increase of 102.5 percent, but this was an absolute

noncompetitiveness of Eastern European and Soviet manufacturers with those of Western Europe, the stress in Communist doctrine on building national self-sufficiency, the disinclination of Communist doctrine to appreciate the principles of comparative advantage and international specialization, the unattractiveness of Eastern European foodstuffs for an EEC already plagued by agricultural subsidy problems, and the difficulties the Eastern Europeans have encountered until recently in securing from the West long-term credits for purchases.

Current changes in Eastern European and Soviet national economic policies should favor expansion of trade with Western Europe in the 1970s. A greater inclination to provide private-consumption goods should call attention to the immediately available supplies in Western Europe. A growing concern with improving the efficiency of resource allocation should lead the WTO governments to appreciate the productivity-increasing effects which a greatly expanded foreign trade based on comparative production advantage would confer on their economies. Privately, the WTO governments have already displayed considerable interest in expanding economic transactions with Western European countries. There is probably more desire for expanded trade and Western technology on the part of Czechoslovakia and Hungary (and all the smaller countries) than in the Soviet Union, which has a special interest in Western investment through special financing arrangements.[5]

Since 1968 the smaller states have been restrained not only by the threats of imminent Russian displeasure implicit in the Brezhnev doctrine but also by the clear assertion of Soviet economic predominance. The FIAT and Mercedes deals, the Ford discussions,

increase of less than 1.5 percentage points. See the background study prepared for the Columbia group by Marilyn Z. Wellons, "Trade of the Federal Republic of Germany with Eastern Europe," on file at the Institute of War and Peace Studies.

[5] See the country-by-country outlook presented by William E. Griffith in "Eastern Europe, Arms Control, and European Security," in Institute of War and Peace Studies, *Arms Control and European Security in the 1970s: Background Papers* (ACDA/IR-152); Report prepared for the U.S. Arms Control and Disarmament Agency, November, 1971; and his earlier study, "Eastern Europe After the Soviet Invasion of Czechoslovakia," (RAND P-3983, October, 1968).

the SU-FGR pipeline agreement, and, even to a degree, the Washington-Moscow trade agreements of 1972 were unquestionably linked to the Russian campaign for a stronger, stricter COMECON, one which would inextricably interweave the Eastern European economies with their own. These efforts have but one clear meaning: fulfillment of Soviet technological and capital requirements must constitute both the primary step toward and the absolute precondition for the improvement of any trade relations between Western and Eastern Europe.

In any case, expanded trade will require more than simply the desire of WTO leaders for it; it will require changing the Communist economies to permit much more flexibility in resource allocation than prevails at present, plus special efforts toward making Eastern goods more competitive in quality with Western goods.

Altogether, one can conclude that over the next decade East-West trade (and other forms of economic cooperation) will grow, but will grow slowly and only in areas sanctioned by Moscow. And because it is currently so small, even if it triples or quadruples in volume, its absolute amount will not be great.

The other part of the question, whether a sizable expansion of interregional trade could affect the security relations between the two regions, can be answered in the negative. Expanding trade is compatible with peaceful relations, but it does not cause them. Expanding trade could be part of an increasing stream of transactions that would do away completely with the division of Europe, but these expanded transactions would have to be generated by political changes within the Communist countries.

II

The answers to the questions posed in the preceding section all point in one direction: whatever the changes in European security arrangements in the 1970s, they will not be *impelled* by changes in economic conditions. With the exception of a fully security-independent Western Europe, a variety of arrangements will be permitted by economic considerations; which ones materialize will depend on military, political, or social forces.

The remainder of this chapter describes prospective political developments in five policy areas central to the future course of European security arrangements: the reorientation of American foreign policy; its consequence for American policy toward Europe; changes in the status of Germany; the development of Soviet policy toward Europe; and trends in Western European domestic and foreign policies.

The authors have found, as have others before them, that the trends and changes that can be discerned in these five areas are less easily delineated than the military and economic developments previously discussed and less pointed in their aggregative effect on future European security arrangements.[6] This is partly because the nature of the political developments involved is more varied, but also because many of these developments are more susceptible to day-to-day changes in the policies and leadership of the United States and other powers.

The Reorientation of American Foreign Policy

The main force that promises to bring changes in American foreign policy is a widely marked phenomenon: an increasingly intense, widespread concern with the backlog of urgent and unresolved problems of domestic life, a call for sacrifice that seems to many persons to be more pressing than any requirements made in the name of asserted "obligations" to world or even allied security. George McGovern's call, "Come home, America," reflected only the American variant of the growing tendency in all developed nations to turn inward and away from the public affairs of

---

[6] The number of studies and model-building exercises concerning European security in the 1970s is by now quite substantial. Among those the ACDA study group found most interesting and useful were Karl E. Birnbaum, *Peace in Europe* (New York: Oxford University Press, 1970); Alastair Buchan, *Europe's Futures, Europe's Choice* (New York: Columbia University Press, 1969); Centre d'Etudes de Politique Etrangère, "Modeles de Sécurité Européene," *Politique Etrangère*, No. 6, 1967, pp. 519–41; Deutsche Gesellschaft für Auswärtige Politik, "Alternativen für Europa: Modelle moglicher Entwicklungen in den siebziger Jahren," *Europa Archiv*, No. 23, 1968, pp. 851–64; Pierre Hassner, "Change and Security in Europe: I and II," *Adelphi Papers*, Nos. 45 and 49 (London: Institute for Strategic Studies, 1968); and Stiftung Wissenschaft und Politik, *Europäische Sicherheit der 70er Jahre* (Ebenhausen, 1968).

the external world, a tendency toward national self-preoccupation.[7] Particularly for the articulate, the influential, and the educated, the primary issues now turn on the quality of national life presently being led and that which will be available to coming generations.

Excessive defense spending is perhaps the clearest focus of this dissent—from the right, the left, and the center. After more than twenty-five years of total diplomacy—nuclear arms competition, military guarantees supported by a huge military establishment deployed overseas, economic and military foreign aid, limited war and cold war—and after the loss of tens of thousands of lives and the expenditure of hundreds of billions of dollars, many Americans in the attentive publics and officialdoms see the world to be no more stable and their lives no more secure than before. Most accept, perhaps grudgingly, a certain level of defense effort as essential to national survival. The critics divide only on what should be done with the extra, excessive resources now commanded by the government. Financial conservatives, for example, would like most of these diverted to the private sector (and thus tax reform becomes tax reduction), whereas many of the vocal young and the poor want the resources retained for public wars on such social ills as poverty, racial tensions, inadequate housing, and pollution.

A clear (and perhaps continuing) manifestation of this trend was the so-called global youth rebellion of recent years.[8] Demonstrations and abortive revolutionary acts expressed youthful discontent with and rejection of the importance for the United States of a national role as a "world policeman," of French national strivings for international "grandeur," and of the supposedly absolute requirements of the defense-minded "metal eaters" in Russia. The conse-

[7] For a more detailed discussion of the Canadian and American experience, see Annette Baker Fox, "Domestic Pressures."

[8] At one point, for example, the incidents of this rebellion commanded more space (4 pages) in the Institute for Strategic Studies' *Strategic Survey: 1969* (London, Institute for Strategic Studies, 1970) than did the Vietnam war (3 pages). Among the expanding literature on the "global" aspects are Barbara and John Ehrenreich, *Long March, Short Spring* (New York: Monthly Review Press, 1969), Donald K. Emmerson (ed.), *Students and Politics in Developing Nations* (London: Pall Mall, 1969), and Sydney Hyman, *Youth in Politics: Expectations and Realities* (New York: Basic Books, 1972).

quences of these beliefs for future adult attitudes and actions are
far from clear. Convincing evidence suggests that such beliefs are
not and were not held by the majority of Americans under thirty
and that increasing age and preoccupation with private affairs will
significantly modify the behavior of some of those now most vocal
and committed.[9] But the broader bases of youthful protest, with
roots in the very nature of affluent societal achievement, cannot be
so easily dismissed and will continue to generate discontent in the
1970s and beyond.

There are limits, however, to the consequences of increasing
preoccupation with domestic problems. As many have recently re-
discovered to their dismay, and some to their relief, every developed system contains major structural constraints against rapid
change, against any immediate radical regrouping of interests and
reallocation of benefits and costs—short, of course, of revolution.
The United States, like the Soviet Union and to a lesser extent the
advanced industrial powers of Western Europe, has foreign-policy
and military-policy elites with sufficient popular support and other
domestic political strength to safeguard a very substantial security
"slice," even in the face of strong competing demands of domestic
problems and pressures for disinvolvement and arms control.[10]

Moreover, the politicians and bureaucrats who will presumably
hold power in Washington and the other major capitals over the
next decade share a heritage of Cold War socialization during
their formative political years.[11] Even the most "liberal" among

[9] One impressionistic account of the Berkeley Free Speech Movement five
years later lends tentative support to this proposition; see Wade Greene,
"Where Are the Savios of Yesteryear," *New York Times Magazine*, July 12,
1970, pp. 6 ff. See also Philip Converse and Howard Schuman's interesting
conclusions concerning significant attitudinal cleavages within the under-thirty
"college" population in their " 'Silent Majorities' and the Vietnam War," *Scientific American*, June, 1970, pp. 22–24.

[10] Certainly this has been the clear experience of Senators seeking curbs on
weapons development in recent years.

[11] See, for example, the arguments advanced by Neal E. Cutler in "Genera-
tional Succession as a Source of Foreign Policy Attitudes," *Journal of Peace
Research* (Oslo), 1970, pp. 33–47; and by Karl Mannheim, "The Sociological
Problem of Generations" in Paul Kecskemeti (ed.), *Essays on the Sociology of
Knowledge* (New York: Oxford University Press, 1952), pp. 276–322.

them will still be significantly influenced by past national security problems and fears, and most will continue to regard relatively high levels of military spending and defense effort as normal and perhaps unavoidable, if not appropriate. Accordingly, Vietnam termination and SALT Phase I will at most result in minor decreases and reallocations within present budgetary demands. A major reduction in national security expenditures will have to wait on events perceived as providing significant, radical improvements in the external political environment.

Nonetheless, whether one looks at Washington or the country, there seems every reason to expect over the next decade changes in America's global commitments, both in the level of its involvement and in the priority assigned to the security of various regions of the world. As the painful task of terminating the Vietnam war has proceeded, the United States has begun to draw back from the Asian mainland, loud in its reaffirmation of its commitments and its pledge to provide assistance under the Nixon Doctrine, but determined once again not to be bogged down in another Korea or another Vietnam. Those in both parties who consistently sought a basic contraction of the American role in Asia have become stronger and more numerous. Quite apart from the future course of American-Chinese relations, the maximum "acceptable" involvement may well be an "off-shore" Asian role, i.e., strong ties with Japan, Australia, New Zealand, and other states coupled with a basic definition of a naval presence and corresponding exclusion of a United States role on the Asian mainland. And there has certainly been renewed interest in finding Asian "replacements"—the prominent solution being the affluent, noninvolved Japanese—to assume balance-maintaining responsibilities.

This "Asia-lationism" will reflect a downward trend in the share of attention and resources that America devotes to the problems of the less-developed countries. With the exception of the Middle East, there is no need to assume that any part of the non-Western world will necessarily pose a major security problem for the United States during the 1970s. Moreover, the Vietnam experience has clearly raised domestic resistance to all forms of intervention and to a continuing "peacekeeping presence" in new places, except under circumstances of direct, unmistakable threat to the United States itself.

It should be stressed that shifts in attention, commitment, and level of acceptable involvement are normal aspects of any American postwar adjustment. Moreover, the lessons of Vietnam will probably turn out to be no more durable a guide for American foreign policy than were the lessons of World War I or the Korean War. Man has lost neither his propensity to differ in his conception of the proper political order nor his propensity to use force to change that order. Accordingly, the combination of some continued adversary relationship among the United States, the Soviet Union, and China, coupled with the explosive tinder of the less-developed world's losing battle with people, poverty, and hunger, could well produce before the decade's end a crisis which will seem to undo the lessons of Vietnam. But barring this, the decade seems most likely to witness a significant reduction in the level of and a narrowing in the scope of American global concerns.

The primary external focuses, therefore, will be Western Europe and the Soviet Union, with the latter assuming even greater predominance than during the late 1960s. Although much of "convergence" theory will remain wishful thinking, continuing understandings and the discovery of new areas where superpower interests are at least complementary will provide new support for Washington's search for détente and will strengthen interest in a limited-adversary relationship. But even if such superpower agreements are minimal and the arms race beyond SALT I continues unchecked, American decision-makers will continue to expect (and hope for) an expansion of political dialogue and of areas of limited cooperation with the Soviet Union—as presumably will their opposite numbers.

American Policy Toward Europe

The effect of these new American policy orientations on Europe will be somewhat more complex than in the case of Asia or even of the Soviet Union. On the one hand, Western European predominance in a shrinking American world view will result in increased attention to European affairs and in more frequent and more consequential consultations with European leaders. On the other hand, the size of American forces on the Continent will almost certainly be reduced by the mid-1970s, and the debate that will accompany the size and timing of this reduction is bound to strain the relations between the United States and its allies. A modest reduction will not satisfy those Americans who believe the prosperous Western Europeans should do more to provide for their own defense. A major reduction will alarm those Europeans who believe that a few American divisions would provide insufficient assurance of continuing protection against Russian (or German) misbehavior or of automatic engagement of American nuclear power in the hour of need. And a reduction of any size will be seen as counterproductive by those on both sides of the Atlantic who doubt that the Americans by doing less can compel the Europeans to do more.

Whatever the change in the size of the military presence in Europe, the basic American commitment to Western European defense—and therefore the basic nuclear guarantee—is quite unlikely to change.[12] Even with a growing American unwillingness to risk a thermonuclear exchange, the United States will find it difficult to close its nuclear umbrella over Western Europe and perhaps even more difficult to make either its allies or the Soviet Union believe that the umbrella finally and firmly has been closed. With men on both sides of the Atlantic thinking of each other as part of "us," Americans will not easily contemplate the prospect of standing aside in the hour of Western Europe's crisis. And the consequence of such action for American credibility both globally and in Moscow, as well as the long-run implications of losing the European resource base, will not be ignored.

In contrast to Western Europe, American policy toward Eastern Europe, given the primacy accorded superpower détente and the general lowering of American external sights, will be one of lessened concern. While continuing its low-keyed improvement of trade and cultural ties, Washington in the 1970s will be more

[12] See Annette Baker Fox's conclusions in "NATO and the American Nuclear Deterrent," *European Security and the Atlantic System.*

acutely and consistently aware of the inherent contradictions between pursuing détente with the Soviet Union and building
bridges to the Eastern European states. It will therefore assume a
low-profile posture, leaving the initiative to allied states (as with
Bonn's Eastern thrust) so long as its ultimate stakes in the German
question and a future European settlement remain untouched.

The structure of NATO in the 1970s will almost certainly reflect
lessening fears of overt Soviet military action. Perhaps the only
fixed American requirement for a Western security organization is
participation by at least three of the Western European Big Four,
with the smaller powers having as much or as little access as they
wish. (If any other major power were to follow the French example, one could hardly still speak of a "Western" security organization.) The broad framework of an American-guaranteed Europe
could permit, for example, both a continued neutral stance by the
efficiently defended Swedes and Swiss and more local international
arrangements for security by smaller NATO members neither
equipped nor disposed to share in the defense of distant parts of
the NATO area.[13]

Should—as is likely—the United States fail to respect the wishes
of lesser powers either for access to or for limits on participation in
Western security organizations, this might well release long pent-
up demands for change in existing "unresponsive" organizational
forms. As the Canadian decision to disengage partially demonstrated, disintegration can be a consequence of clinging to international security organizations perceived as obsolete, rigid, and in-
sensitively centralized.[14] It already may have become far easier
and less costly to pay simple lip service to traditional forms while
effectively reducing national efforts than to persevere in the hope
that time and relatively good behavior will bring changes in
Washington's opposition to reductions in force.

[13] See Birnbaum, *Peace in Europe;* and Nils Ørvik, "NATO and the Regional Approach to European Security" in Istvan Szent-Miklosy (ed.), *Studies
for a New Central Europe,* 1968/1969 (Series 3, Nos. 3/4), pp. 274–82.

[14] See Mrs. Fox's discussion of the background of the Canadian move in
"Domestic Pressures" and the more general treatment of disintegrative tenden-
cies in Francis A. Beer, *Integration and Disintegration in NATO* (Columbus:
Ohio State University Press, 1969).

Indeed, if NATO is to continue in any recognizable form, the crucial factor will be Washington's willingness to be both attentive and responsive to Continental demands—specifically, to give its allies the access to the American decision-making process they believe they require. Since this is an area with a very limited depoliticization potential, mere demonstration of the superior expertise in the military technology on which American policy positions were said to be based has never convinced NATO partners that their interests were being well served. And for those allies who will count most—Britain, France, and Germany—effective influence means sharing in deliberations far beyond those narrowly defined as military.

Insistence on an exclusive American nuclear veto, combined with Soviet-American arms control agreements which even indirectly affect Continental deployments (let alone forward-based tactical nuclear systems) would constitute only the most obvious example of such unresponsiveness. But failure to move further in creating new and more responsive organizational forms—whether on a bilateral or multilateral basis—probably will lead not so much to the intensification of national efforts or the emergence of a separate Western European security organization as to inaction, immobility, and the disintegration of the existing Atlantic organization.

The Status of Germany

The division between the two Germanies can be expected to persist throughout the 1970s. Whenever and under whatever rubric West German recognition finally occurs, relations with East Germany will become increasingly more "normalized" and will involve greater and easier interstate contacts and interchange on all levels, official and private. But that the new East German leaders or their possible successors will prove radically more interested in serious consultation and cooperation seems at best questionable. At issue for the post-Ulbricht leadership are not only their personal political stakes but also their structural interest in separation—in terms of the German Democratic Republic's role both globally and within the Communist commonwealth.[15] As the Brandt-Scheel government implicitly acknowledged on its accession, there was virtually no West German price short of capitulation (even if it could be offered by Bonn) which in 1970 would have assured immediate reunification. By 1980 the prospects will be even slimmer.

Nor can the Soviet Union be expected to take such initiatives, even after its open intervention in the interests of a swift conclusion of the Berlin Agreements. The division of Germany remains a prime object of Soviet foreign policy. Despite the recent warming trends in German-Soviet relations, it is clear that Soviet political interest still lies at least partially in making continued common anti-German cause with both Eastern and Western Europeans. At a minimum, this insures responsiveness to the Soviet political-military effort to dominate one half of Europe and divide the other. In comparison, the payoffs from a thoroughgoing Bonn-Moscow rapprochement or perhaps a second Rapallo would seem less significant, even if continued division of Germany is assured.[16]

The major question in the case of West Germany is the extent to which it can become a fully accepted partner and even a leader of the other Western European countries in the 1970s. The primary constraint upon such a rehabilitation will be the persisting predispositional barriers among those European generations and nationalities with particular anti-German outlooks based on past unhappy experiences. Without question, considerable progress has already been achieved (most startlingly perhaps in Holland and Britain), and the recent record of an untainted, Socialist-led coalition can only help.[17] But both historical memory and future power

[15] See David Child's brief but provoking discussion of the "Red Jesuits' " motives and goals in *East Germany* (New York: Frederick A. Praeger, 1969), Chs. II and XII, and Peter Bender's very different findings in *Eastern Europe in Search of Security* (Baltimore: The Johns Hopkins Press, 1972).

[16] Nonetheless, Soviet leaders have always seen value in a "stick but also carrot" approach to the Germans in hopes of heightening internal dissent, of hastening self-isolation from the West, and—particularly since 1968—of exploiting West Germany's financial resources. On this subject see Wolfram F. Hanrieder, *The Stable Crisis* (New York: Harper & Row, 1970), Chapter III; and Thomas W. Wolfe, *Soviet Power and Europe, 1945–1970* (Baltimore: The Johns Hopkins Press, 1970).

[17] Press reports suggest that this purity may have been one of the factors

calculations will be enough to sustain the basic belief that those who populate the precarious center of Europe must be watched, and watched carefully.

A continuing cause for concern will be the relative size and armament of West German armed forces, which now are and probably will continue to be the largest and best equipped of the Western European contingents. Economic indicators provide no basis for Bonn's emergence in the 1970s as a formidable military power dangerous to all other European countries or dominant in an integrated Europe. West Germany's population is only a little more than one-quarter of the Soviet population, and its economic-military potential is at most only one-third of the Soviets'. Although the West German potential somewhat exceeds that of either Britain or France, West German GNP and population are only about one-quarter of those of the original six EEC countries and Britain combined. Thus, as long as all the larger European countries continue to transform a roughly equal proportion of their economic potential into organized military strength, West Germany could not become a threat to the security of Europe by virtue of her military power, nor could she dominate an integrated Western Europe.[18]

A reduction in American military forces in Europe, however, would heighten West Germany's present predominance in NATO divisions on the Central European front—a fact well understood by Bonn—even if West Germany should reduce its forces to the occasionally discussed levels of eight or even six full-strength divisions.[19] And fewer Americans for guard and stockpile duty automatically raises the question of "German" tactical nuclear weapons —for Bonn, in terms of their assured delivery for German launch-

---

easing Brandt's assumption of leadership at the 1969 and 1972 EEC summit meetings. See, for example, the tone of *The Economist's* special section "Willy Brandt's Inheritance," January 10, 1970.

[18] See Klaus Knorr. "Economic Factors in Future Arrangements for European Security, *Arms Control and European Security in the 1970s: Background Papers* (ACDA/IR-152), section V.

[19] A Defense White Paper published in 1970 did not foresee any such cuts during the subsequent three-year planning period (Bonn: Bundespresseamt, 1970.) See also the statements of the then Opposition defense spokesman, Helmut Schmidt, in his *The Balance of Power* (London: William Kimber, 1971), especially Chapter IX.

ers in time of conflict; and for both Western and Eastern Europeans, in terms of unauthorized German access or even a resulting push toward national weapons control or development.

Despite these problems and lingering resentments, West Germany, so long as it remains a rich and powerful part of an irremediably divided country, with a quarter-century record of reasonable behavior and cooperation, will increasingly assume during the 1970s a leading (and in some areas *the* leading) Western role. There are a number of reasons why West Germany with its *Ostpolitik* may continue to be on the cutting edge of Western efforts to improve Eastern European relations: the attractiveness of the West German economic and technological bargaining list, and the inward-drawing concerns of other states, to name only two. In the absence of a revived French interest in leadership and an effective, accepted British role in Europe, Bonn may also be the source of most expansion initiatives within the EEC for some time to come.[20]

A somewhat parallel development in East Germany's role in the Communist world can be expected. As the Czechoslovak crisis dramatically reemphasized, the East German government is less than popular among the Communist states because of its ideological orthodoxy, its smug prosperity, its constant currying of Moscow's favor, its Germanness. Yet, as the eighth industrial power in the world, East Germany clearly constitutes an available source of much-needed capital and technological assistance. And as a state in existence for more than twenty years, with a leadership displaying both tactical sophistication and at least a minimum degree of popular support, it represents the Communist world's insurance against German-caused instability in Central Europe.[21]

A major consequence of both Germanies' rehabilitation will be

[20] The most European of all present German political leaders (in at least the verbal sense) is, of course, Franz Josef Strauss, who is currently the loudest (if not strongest) voice of the Christian Democratic Union–Christian Social Union opposition. For the most recent version of his European proposals, see his *Challenge and Response* (London: Weidenfeld and Nicolson, 1969), especially chapter X.

[21] See William E. Griffith, "Eastern Europe, Arms Control, and European Security."

to diminish further the German threat as even a partial stimulus toward regional security cooperation. Clearly, it will be less and less possible to maintain even the much-faded role of this argument in justifying organizational attempts in the West (e.g., the continued inviolable large foreign-force deployments in the Federal Republic); and although the effects in the East are less certain, the ambivalence of Soviet policy should emerge in even sharper relief.

Reduced apprehension about Germany will help to stabilize East-West relations in Europe in several ways. It will lay to rest fears that the division between "our Germans" and "your Germans" might be ending. It will take the political profit out of proposals—whether from Moscow, Washington, or any interested European politician, Eastern or Western—that play on hopes and fears about German reunification and the "lost territories." Finally, when and if relations between the two Germanies are formalized, the formalization will seem a less provocative and value-laden event for both populations.

Such stabilization, however, will only make the thornier, unresolved aspects of the German question more apparent. *Ostpolitik* or not, as the Brandt-Scheel government painfully learned, no leadership of the Federal Republic of Germany during the 1970s and perhaps in the 1980s can seem to turn its back on "the brothers and sisters in the East" as long as complete intra-German normalization does not occur. Bonn will have to be sensitive to and potentially blackmailable with respect to their fate, in either human or political terms. Thus there is always the threat of instability in West Germany's own relations with the East and in East-West relations that it tries to lead or for which it is a convenient conduit.

Moreover, the fact of division will continue to exert an unsettling influence on domestic political debate. One cannot assume that because the Federal Republic seems to have developed an effective two-party system, an Anglo-Saxon-like consensus is also the norm on important issues of domestic or foreign policy. Given the type of irresponsibility which the postwar political system allows parties and individuals to display at little cost and with considerable hope of gain (e.g., the role taken by Strauss and the

Christian Social Union during the debates on the Moscow and Warsaw agreements, as on the earlier nonproliferation treaty), there will probably continue to be the constant threat of a lurch, of a major foreign policy retrenchment, however unlikely or unrealistic this might seem from an objective perspective.[22]

And no hard evidence suggests that even the recent strides with respect to the guaranteed status of West Berlin—for the 1950s and the 1960s, both the symbol and the flash point of the German question—will set off a chain of further agreements or be of great long-run significance. Berlin's security will still be assured—as it has been for the last twenty years—by the fact of physical American-Soviet confrontation in Central Europe and by the symbolic value both sides have come to accord any escalatory or potentially disruptive action. The primary gain in the Berlin accords lay in gaining at least this first measure of basic agreement among the wartime allies and the two Germanies despite highly complex negotiation procedures (the intermeshing of talks on three distinct levels) and repeated East German (and some West German) foot-dragging. The meaningful long-range answers to the political and economic questions which have always been encapsulated in the issue of Berlin's continued viability still would seem to require binding decisions on the direction and rate of an all-European settlement. And the probability of substantial progress toward such an explicit agreement before 1980 is difficult to calculate.

Soviet Policy Toward Europe

The Soviet Union may share some of the growing American interest in giving higher priority to domestic needs and programs, especially in light of its problems in adapting previous patterns of party and bureaucratic management to the post-industrial technology, but at the moment the basic thrust of Soviet policy is not inward but outward. As the United States is poised to disengage from the less-developed world, the Soviet Union is moving into the

---

[22] The West German Federal election campaign of 1972 and the fateful Bundestag debates on ratification of the Moscow and Warsaw agreements offer ample evidence of such political irresponsibility (e.g., "Brandt is playing the game of the Kremlin"), backed by few discernible alternative proposals for foreign policy or by objective opportunities for policy change.

Mediterranean, the Indian Ocean, and Southeast Asia. If the Pentagon is increasingly hard pressed, Soviet military programs and leaders seem rather to be in the ascendancy. And if Americans now see the ending of their Asian conflict, the Soviets by no means see the end of theirs.

But although the outward thrust of Soviet policy seems clear, it is far from evident what Soviet leaders hope or expect to achieve from these initiatives. What, for example, lies behind the intensive campaign of the past few years for a European security conference? Has the Soviet Union seized on the widespread desire for European détente as a means to promote certain tactical objectives (the recognition of the East German state, the legitimation of the Brezhnev doctrine)? Or—as many Europeans have come to hope —has the Soviet Union made a strategic decision, particularly in light of its conflict with China, to seek more stable and ordered relations on its European flank, relations which would permit Western and Eastern Europeans to enjoy more autonomy in their relations with their respective superpower ally and more normal relations between themselves?

Some observers, especially those who cherish the conspiracy theory of history, are inclined to view all current Soviet diplomatic moves—whether in SALT or at Geneva, whether in trade talks with Washington or mutual nonaggression pledges with Bonn, whether regarding a Middle East settlement or the Security conference itself—as simply temporizing moves until the Soviet Union can gain decisive strategic superiority in the late 1970s or until the United States, impelled by internal dissent, abandons its postwar leadership role and retreats into neo-isolationism. Most observers, however, stress the need for a more complex interpretation that includes at a minimum the recognition that Soviet leaders and their political-bureaucratic constituents are neither completely united in their objectives nor wholly confident in their sense of how best to achieve those objectives.[23]

[23] This and the discussion that follows are indebted to the ideas advanced by Wolfe in *Soviet Power and Europe*, Chs. 12–15, and by Marshall Shulman in "Soviet Proposals For A European Security Conference 1966–1969," *Arms Control and European Security in the 1970s: Background Papers* (ACDA/ IR-152).

What is clear is that in Europe the Soviet leaders do confront a painful dilemma with regard to the Brezhnev doctrine. Although they have the capacity to physically dominate Eastern Europe, they cannot in the long run maintain centralized control over the political and economic policies of those states while simultaneously insuring the economic progress and technological adaptation that the peoples of Eastern Europe urgently demand. But to fail to assure vigorous economic development is to court recurring political instability in Eastern Europe, and to engage in repeat performances of August 1968 is to invite mounting losses not only in Eastern European allegiance but also possibly in Soviet domestic support and most certainly in Western confidence in Moscow's lack of interest in using force elsewhere in Europe.

Indeed, whatever the more distant European security outcomes, the 1970s are likely to be characterized by continued stirrings and strivings toward greater relative autonomy on both sides of the Continent's division. As a result, the relations of the Soviet Union with its European allies (similar to those of the United States) will continue to be caught in the strain inherent in Soviet interest in both a high degree of alliance cohesion and discipline and a lessening of the risk of superpower conflict through mutual, assured, sufficient nuclear deterrence. The more effective the strategic ceiling, the lower may be the expectation of violence in Europe, and thus the greater the temptation for middle and small powers on both sides to try to evade their share of the security burden and to probe, with low risk and some benefit, the limits of their major ally's (and perhaps their major opponent's) tolerance for quasi-autonomous policy.

Nonetheless, moved by the dictates of political orthodoxy and the persistent fear of a resurgent Germany (allied to and thereby potentially capable of ensnaring the United States in German pursuits), the Soviet Union will continue to see its security as seriously compromised by any policies which foreshadow a loosening of its dominance over or an increase of Western influence in the northern tier states—East Germany, Poland, and Czechoslovakia—and probably in Hungary and Bulgaria as well. And although the Soviets will undoubtedly continue to give rhetorical support to Western European hopes for more normal relations with Eastern Europe, they will also continue to view with great suspicion (if not to meet with direct resistance) any movement toward more formal organization of shared economic or political interests that would threaten to move relations between the two Europes beyond their control.

A second near certainty is that the Soviet Union will not halt its efforts to divide and to exploit divisions among the Western states. Since the Soviet Union is deemed ideologically irrelevant by most of the major radical fomenters of Western domestic turbulence, there will be little opportunity to recruit active allies among the young or the alienated in the West. A more profitable tactic, especially if future developments in American foreign policy appear to promise a partial disintegration of the political and military institutions of the North Atlantic alliance, will be to encourage neutralist trends in Western European governments through ardent bilateral wooing in the name of détente and general European security.

As in the past, the main effort will be to isolate (and thereby to neutralize) the West Germans—if not from Washington, at least from London and Paris. The tactics will be the familiar carrot and stick, with incentives tailored for the 1970s—the continuing expansion of trade and cultural relations, the glittering prospect of future joint developments in Siberia, the hope of continuing Soviet pressure to ameliorate East German rigidities, and Soviet permission for widened relations with other Eastern European countries.

In light of these two near certainties, Soviet proposals for a European security conference would seem to reflect more an ambition to use a new vehicle to reach old objectives than a serious interest in exploring a new order for European security. Moreover, to the extent that Soviet leaders are drawn to the desirability of reaching an agreement with the United States on Europe, the result will certainly subordinate the Western and Eastern European concept of a no longer divided Europe to the superpower vision of Big Two détente—a controlled, exclusive, limited-adversary relationship, with some of the limits agreed to at the expense of their respective European allies.

Western European Domestic and Foreign Policies

The considerations that point to a shift in American political priorities from national security problems to domestic affairs would seem to be even more influential in the case of Western Europe. The nations of Western Europe have basically completed their disengagement from non-Western problems; there is not much they can do about the stability of the nuclear balance; and the progressive downgrading of the threat of a Soviet attack has eased fears about their own security and hence reduced the importance of relations with the superpowers. There is really very little left for them to do except to concern themselves with the problems of mounting affluence and their relations with each other.

One result of this shift in attention could be an increased movement toward the left. In the recent past, such shifts have resulted from a weariness with the Cold War conflicts of the last two decades and from social-democratic aspirations. Where this movement resulted in the establishment of Left-leaning, welfare-minded governments, these governments, even when remaining formally committed to the Atlantic security community, have been gravely tempted to cut back on or opt out of what they saw as marginal defense activities, primarily their investments in the conventional-defense area.[24] In the future, the principal trends will almost certainly include an end to conscription and to mass armies in general, a setting of smaller or fixed budgetary levels for military spending, and even a backing away from most high-technology investment in conventional equipment. Those who do not remain formally committed and adopt a more neutralistic posture will undoubtedly deny that the threat from the East is essentially greater than the threat from the West.

The trends which produce a movement inward may not of course result in government by and for the Left; in some countries it is almost equally probable that they may lead to the right.[25] In

[24] This of course will be a continuation of the trends of the late 1960s. See, for example, the figures in U.S. Arms Control and Disarmament Agency, *World Military Expenditures 1969*, Table IV, p. 17.

[25] See on this point Karl Kaiser and Roger Morgan (eds.), *Britain and West*

Britain such developments were one of the prime bases for the Tory return to power. In West Germany (as in other states) a conservative or Rightist law-and-order reaction to the student unrest of the late 1960s coupled with difficulties with the United States, residual anxieties concerning the pursuit of *Ostpolitik,* and primary fears about a leveling-off in the pursuit of affluence is quite conceivable. However, because of the desire of its supporters for tax reductions, a Right government's policies may run in the same direction as those of a Left government: principally toward reductions in defense expenditures.

The most likely outcome in all European states is a Left-Center coalition. The Left can provide the governmental dynamism and can demand as its due some movement leftward in internal affairs, with important consequences for foreign policy. But if the Left (or similarly, the Right) wishes to govern at all, the experience of the 1960s suggests it must remain in a coalition of mutual necessity with Center elements of public opinion, which will hold the balance in all European (indeed, at present in all developed) systems. This alone might seem an effective barrier to radical policy reorientation, a strong force for both continuity and depoliticization in foreign policy as well as in domestic sectors.

But the inherent tendency of such past coalitions to take the least disruptive path for the sake of remaining in power may well reinforce the trend toward self-preoccupation through increased measures of individual alienation. The professed ideals of greater citizen participation in political life and of governmental decentralization and simplification in the interests of finally realizing the European democratic revolution will stand in sharp contrast to "bureaucratic politics as usual" and the endorsement of change only with "deliberate and considered" speed.[26]

There seems, then, more than a substantial chance that by the end of the 1970s most of the Western European states will have

Germany: Changing Societies and the Future of Foreign Policy (London and New York: Oxford University Press, 1971).

[26] See Jean-Jacques Servan-Schreiber, *The Spirit of May* (New York: McGraw-Hill Book Company, 1969); Andre Fontaine, *La Guerre Civile Froide* (Paris: Fayard, 1969) for two "moderate" assessments of the relevant French experience.

turned inward, making them even less interested in sacrifice in support of an effective Atlantic security organization and more committed to a policy of détente. At a minimum, this will provide a plausible basis for cutting defense expenditures and thereby permit not only increased welfare expenditures but minimum attention to extra-European affairs in general.

Western European regional cooperation remains, however, a potentially major foreign-policy preoccupation that could offset some of the developments described above. The point was made in Section I that if the nations of Western Europe were to make significant progress toward economic and political union in the 1970s, the impetus would have to be new, major, and basically political. At present, the basis for a prediction of greater integration seems slight. Many of the original motives for European union no longer have political relevance: to build a basis for economic prosperity, to unite against the Communist menace, to create the means for exercising an independent world role. Most of the original ideological leaders (men like Adenauer, Schuman, and De Gasperi) have passed from the scene, leaving behind neither new leaders with equally strong European orientations nor many prominent enthusiasts among the younger, more pragmatic generations. Indeed, many of the most politically active European youths would oppose "building a Europe," so long as that Europe would represent only a consolidation of the political, economic, and social order they hold in disdain.

Any decisive movement toward an effective economic and political union in the 1970s will have to be a joint effort by all three major Western European powers: Britain, France, and Germany. But the initiative seems unlikely to come from any of them. The West Germans can hardly take the lead, lest they be suspect of striving once again for hegemony. This seemingly will be true even if no explicit commitment to the development of a security community is involved and the cost to German prosperity (the highest consensual value) is minimized. The two dominant parties in France, the Gaullists and the Communists, are both opposed to comprehensive European integration. And Britain must have emerged from its status as a new boy in the EEC—perhaps by taking an even clearer stand against the earlier and still popular Washingtonian, Commonwealth, or "Little England" foreign-policy orientations—before it can begin a frontal (and improbable) attack on the present limited arrangements.[27]

Lacking political direction and having no overwhelming economic motivation, the European Nine—or more probably by 1980 an even larger Community group—will continue the slow, problem-by-problem approach of the past toward greater regional cooperation. Their approach to the problems caused by developments in nonmilitary technology is typical. The limits set by national firms and markets, along with lesser problems like outmoded management practices and attitudes and inadequate communications and electric power networks, have prevented Western European producers from taking full advantage of many existing technologies. The inclusion of Britain, the Western European country with the strongest scientific and technological capability, in the EEC will help complete the process of achieving a large market, but the problem of amassing resources for research, development, and production on the scale required by the new technology will remain. Indeed, many of the most important technological innovations expected during the next decade (cheaper energy production, improved communication and transportation means, utilization of ocean-floor resources) will require even larger than heretofore scales of development and production and thus larger markets and capital investments.[28]

Union of the Western European economies would obviously provide a final solution. But if Western European countries can find less disrupting means of permitting utilization of new technological

[27] These paragraphs have been paraphrased from Klaus Knorr, "Economic Factors in Future Arrangements for European Security." See also Catherine M. Kelleher and Donald J. Puchala, "Germany, European Security, and Arms Control"; Wilfrid L. Kohl, "France and European Security: De Gaulle and After"; and Andrew J. Pierre, "Britain and European Security: Issues and Choices for the 1970s," especially Part I, all in *European Security and the Atlantic System.* Some of the nuances and the graceful "outs" provided by the then Opposition leader, Edward Heath, in his article, "Realism in British Foreign Policy," *Foreign Affairs,* October, 1969, pp. 39–50, are also interesting.

[28] See Victor Basiuk, "Future Technology and Western European Security," in *European Security and the Atlantic System.*"

developments, they can be expected to choose them, and they are already doing so.[29] Conventions concerning "European" patents and the operations of multinational firms have been drafted; a company to supply venture capital for technology-based firms has been established; efforts to devise uniform industrial standards are being made; and young executives with American training and attitudes are more and more in control of European managements. Considerable success seems assured, since a burgeoning nonmilitary technology does not require, for example, the common monetary and fiscal policy necessary for economic union or the unified development effort needed to attain a major nuclear-deterrent capability.[30]

European cooperation in conventional military technology will be limited, however. The advantages to be gained through economies of scale and a multinational market are obvious, but as in the development of an independent nuclear capability previously discussed, the Western Europeans will almost certainly be unable to reap these benefits until they develop a central political framework for resolving inter-military and inter-nation disagreements about the distribution of the risks, costs, and benefits involved in joint weapons development projects.[31] Although joint efforts in certain

[29] This is of course a primary indictment of the European approach to technology—even on a national level—made by Jean-Jacques Servan-Schreiber in *The American Challenge* (New York: Atheneum, 1968) and Aurelio Peccei in *The Chasm Ahead* (New York: Macmillan Company, 1969). See also Victor Basiuk's discussion in "Future Technology.

[30] There will of course be much greater chance of success, Victor Basiuk suggests, if the Europeans create an all-Europe patent system and institutions to provide huge fixed-return loans and eventually perhaps transfer national efforts to existing European scientific-technological organizations (ELDO, ESRO, Euratom, CERN) reorganized within a future European Space Agency and an European Nuclear Power Authority. See "Future Technology."

[31] The most detailed examinations of the potential magnitude of these benefits can be found in the Institute for Strategic Studies' definitive series, *Defence, Technology and the Western Alliance* (London: 1967), especially in C. J. E. Harlow, "The European Armament Base" (II, Parts 1 and 2), and Robert R. James, "Standardization and Common Production of Weapons in NATO" (III). See the latter, pp. 9–19, for an account of the factors that have undermined or caused the failure of such bilateral and multilateral projects as the Fiat G-91, the *Atlantique*, the F-104G "Starfighter," the Leopard, and the Hawk.

areas (e.g., the European combat aircraft, the British-Dutch-German limited efforts with nuclear centrifuge technology) will remain attractive, declining growth rates may make the economic spillover effects of national military production seem more valuable and attractive. As for nuclear weapons, unless Britain and France revise current plans or actively pursue an unlikely Europeanization program, by 1975 there will be a significant degradation of even the present limited European nuclear-production base. Not only will the existing national forces be subject to rapid obsolescence but the basic support industries will require major infusions of investment capital and basic research and development inputs (domestic or imported).[32] Even the development by 1980 of an impressive European scientific-technological capability could only mitigate the short-run effects of this degradation.

Perhaps the greatest impetus toward Western European regional cooperation will come from year-in, year-out accretions of expert interchange and from transnational bureaucratization of government policy. What this involves is the process of depoliticization —the tendency to entrust to experts the comanagement with opposite-number experts of problems politically defined as shared.[33] Operating with general guidelines, these experts can create a body of practice and detailed agreement which, as General de Gaulle well understood, can reduce any one member government's day-

[32] Advances in civilian nuclear technology expected in the 1980s with the introduction of efficient "fast breeder" technology will make independent plutonium production much easier and cheaper. But the basic problems of force modernization will remain—warhead miniaturization, missile-guidance improvement for increased accuracy and control, the development (or purchase) of MIRV technology, and follow-ons for the Polaris system and MRBMs. See Kohl, "France and European Security" and Pierre, "Britain and European Security."

[33] Carried to its extreme, this argument approaches that advanced by the extreme "functionalist" school, which is best summarized by Walter Hallstein's comment: "What is emerging from all this is not just economic union. Rather it is political union limited to the economic and social fields. . . . The logic of economic integration . . . leads on towards political unity by way of the fusion of economic interests." Quoted in (and challenged by) W. Horsfall Carter, "A Hard Look at the Community," *International Affairs*, April, 1970, p. 286.

On the experts themselves, see Arturo Spinelli, *The Eurocrats* (Baltimore: The Johns Hopkins Press, 1966).

to-day freedom of action, even in the management of acute international crises. Furthermore, when opposite-number ministers meet regularly, as in NATO and the EEC, they tend to develop shared expectations, habits of common action, and an esprit to support that action.

The institution-building euphoria of the 1950s clearly has been dissipated by the discovery of the 1960s that such trends can be reversed at little cost at any time, that unilateral sabotage or reduction of effort can cause reverse spillover effects. Yet the 1970s will see a continuation of the depoliticization and denationalization of certain kinds of intra-Western relations through limited-purpose organizations of varying membership and progress through occasional spurts of limited goal setting (e.g., the October 1972 summit meeting). To take only the most pressing near-future example: there is a high probability that the 1970s will see a comprehensive Western agreement (perhaps among the Financial Ten) on cooperative monetary and fiscal policies, to be administered by an international body relatively shielded from day-to-day national pressures.[34] Despite its centrality for continued Western prosperity, such an agreement will not, in and of itself, foster greater political cooperation on the related matters of trade regulation or social welfare credits. In these areas, as in that of European security, its effect can only be permissive: it will remove one stumbling block to greater cooperation that may (or may not) be desired on its own merits.

In summary: relations among the Western European states will continue to be friendly, and increasing cooperation can be expected in limited-purpose organizations. But no degree of success in these limited-purpose spheres (whether economic, political, or military) will involve automatic spillover into any other sphere or even further intensification of efforts within that sphere. After an initial shakedown period has passed, the addition of three new members to the EEC will surely result in new coalitions and lead-

---

[34] For an interesting short review of what has been achieved already and what has yet to be achieved, see Etienne-Sadi Kirschen (with Henry S. Bloch and William B. Bassett), *Financial Integration in Western Europe* (New York: Columbia University Press, 1969).

ership patterns, with a potential two-to-one division among London, Bonn, and Paris on key Community issues.[35] The extent of this political and economic cooperation will fall far short, however, of what would be required for truly effective coordination of Western European national security policies.

The only major external preoccupations of the Western European states will be relations with the superpowers, and even these will be of an intermittent character. With the Soviet Union, the principal interest will be trade and normalization. With the United States, relations are likely to follow the pattern of the late 1960s—more detached criticism, harder bargaining, and a greater emphasis on bilateral rather than multilateral negotiations and arrangements. Within this context, the only real alternatives for Western Europe's defense effort in the 1970s lie in the range between something like the present magnitude of effort and something significantly less.

The prospect in the 1970s, then, is for a Europe that is characterized as much by individual national efforts and domestic preoccupations as by joint, externally oriented endeavors and new unions, whether for security or any other regional purpose. The only impetus that could change this prospect is extra-European: the highly improbable combined shock of a disappearing American commitment and a reappearing Soviet threat.

III

The military developments described in Chapter Two threaten the stability of the balance of terror and offer no relief from the strategic dilemma of the 1950s and 1960s. They promise to make

---

[35] See Thomas Barman, "Britain, France, and West Germany: The Changing Pattern of Their Relationship in Europe," *International Affairs,* April, 1970, pp. 269–79; and Alfred Grosser, "France and Germany: Less Divergent Outlooks?" *Foreign Affairs,* January, 1970, pp. 235–44.

For contrasting views on the impact of political changes, see (among many others) J. L. Zaring's persuasive *Decision for Europe: The Necessity of British Engagement* (Baltimore: The Johns Hopkins Press, 1969); and Leon Lindberg and Stuart Scheingold's *Europe's Would-Be Polity* (Englewood Cliffs: Prentice-Hall, 1970).

the control of the arms race both more urgent and more difficult and to place existing European security arrangements under considerable strain. In contrast, the economic developments in prospect in Europe, the United States, and the Soviet Union pose little threat to existing security arrangements and do not by themselves propel movement toward new European security arrangements.

The import of the political and social forces described in the preceding section is not so easily summarized. The forces making for change are quite permissive; they do not all point in the same direction. An attempt to assess the aggregate effect of all of these developments on European security arrangements will obviously be a hazardous and speculative analytical endeavor. This assessment will be deferred until Chapter Six—after developing in Chapter Four the model forms which future European security arrangements might take and examining in Chapter Five the plausibility of pathways that might lead to security arrangements very different from those of 1970.

/ *Chapter Four*

SECURITY ARRANGEMENTS
FOR EUROPE: EIGHT MODELS

I

THE PREVIOUS CHAPTERS have dealt with strategic, military, economic, and sociopolitical factors that the decision-makers of the 1970s can ignore only at their peril. In this chapter the effort to peer ahead takes a different form. Since it is with the aggregate impact of forces making for change that statesmen must cope, this chapter asks "What are the main directions in which the architects of a new Europe can lead or be pushed?" [1]

Three questions may be asked about any set of security arrangements for Europe:

1. Will the line that currently divides Europe persist, with separate security arrangements made for Western Europe and for Eastern Europe?

2. Will both superpowers, only one, or neither continue to be credibly involved in securing the territories of their respective European allies?

---

[1] In this and following chapters, "Europe" refers not to geographic Europe, i.e., that part of Eurasia west of the Urals, but to political Europe, i.e., the European territory that lies between the two superpowers. Thus the Soviet Union is neither more nor less a part of political Europe than is the United States.

3. Will both superpowers, only one, or neither retain a directive role in their present European alliances?

These questions are asked too starkly. The division of Europe may remain significant for some purposes but not for others. The will and capacity of a superpower to protect its present European allies may be self-evident in one set of contingencies and doubtful in another. The directive role of the Soviet Union may be a dictator's role while that of the United States may involve no more than the leadership which accrues to the larger partner when there is basic agreement as to alliance objectives. Yet to ask the questions starkly is to define a number of end-points in imaginable new departures in the security policies of countries with major concerns in Europe.

To regard answers to these three questions as pivotal variables in analyzing Europe's security future is to create a series of limited-characteristic abstractions, ideal-type models useful for analysis even though the security system of the real Europe of the 1970s is far more complex than these abstract models suggest. As Chart 1 indicates, two answers (I, II) are possible to the question about the division of Europe, four (A, B, C, D) to the question regarding credible involvement, and four (1, 2, 3, 4) to the question regarding the directive role of the superpower. Chart 1 indicates the thirty-two formal possibilities that emerge if one combines answers to the three questions in all possible ways. Actually, because there are two significantly different versions of the "autonomous Western Europe, decommitted United States" model (IA1a and IA1b), thirty-three possibilities emerge.

Why, one may ask, are constitutional-organizational arrangements and formal alliances not included as *defining* characteristics of security arrangements? The presence or absence of federal organization in Western Europe sufficient to permit a completely integrated defense and foreign policy for the federation would indeed greatly affect the prospects for a fully autonomous Western Europe. Similarly, a formal treaty commitment provides important if not conclusive evidence of "credible involvement."

It may well be true that the forces leading to a Western Europe powerful enough and self-sacrificing enough to defend itself and efficient in allocating resources for defense would express themselves first by creating supranational regional institutions of genuine political significance. But in the schema used here what is critical is the outcome—the autonomy and defensibility of Western Europe —not the forces and formal institutions which make that outcome possible. Supranational institutions are not defining characteristics in this set of ideal-type outcomes, but dynamic elements which propel Europe toward one or another of these outcomes. In any case, it seems best not to begin by assuming that Western Europe's future is to be described primarily in terms of the rate of its progress toward or away from some grand organizational unity. Similar comments could be made about the Atlantic Community and about a Europe from the Atlantic to the borders of the Soviet Union. Data about supranational organizations and the attitudes which favor or oppose the emergence of particular supranational institutions are, like other data discussed in earlier chapters, treated as input rather than outcome in describing future Europes.

Fortunately, of the thirty-three imagined models of European security arrangements, only eight need to be given more than cursory attention. If the three characteristics—division, involvement, and dominance—were completely independent of one another, each of the thirty-three models might have to be considered; but these defining characteristics are not independent. Many combinations of them are contradictory, some are logically impossible, and others entail political implausibilities. Five kinds of incongruity and implausibility can be distinguished, and by applying these to the thirty-three combinations, all but eight models can be effectively ruled out.

1. A superpower's disengagement from its half of Europe would preclude effective control over the security policies of its European allies. To be in a position to play a dominant role in the security arrangements of its allies a necessary (but not sufficient) condition is a pattern of defense mobilization and military deployment, of treaty commitments and of leadership in coalition diplomatic and military planning that will make the superpower "credibly

Chart 1 Plausible and Implausible Models of Future European Security Arrangements

	I Europe still divided and			
	A U.S.S.R. only involved	B Both involved	C Neither involved	D U.S. only involved
1 U.S.S.R. only dominant	IA1 a BIG SWEDEN W. EUROPE b WEU W. EUROPE	IB1 SHELTERED W. EUROPE	IC1 No divided Europe if neither involved	ID1 No U.S.S.R. dominance without U.S.S.R. involvement
2 Both dominant	IA2 No U.S. dominance without U.S. involvement	IB2 TWO SPHERES EUROPE	IC2 No divided Europe if neither involved	ID2 No U.S.S.R. dominance without involvement
3 Neither dominant	IA3 No divided Europe if neither dominant	IB3 No divided Europe if neither dominant	IC3 No divided Europe if neither dominant and neither involved	ID3 No divided Europe if neither dominant
4 U.S. only dominant	IA4 No U.S. dominance without U.S. involvement	IB4 No sheltered E. Europe if U.S. dominant in W. Europe	IC4 No divided Europe if neither involved	ID4 U.S. disengages if no U.S.S.R. threat and no goal of undivided Europe

II Europe no longer divided; relations between E. and W. Europe normalized and

	A U.S.S.R. only involved	B Both involved	C Neither involved	D U.S. only involved
1 U.S.S.R. only dominant	IIA1 BIG FINLAND W. EUROPE	IIB1 No undivided Europe if both involved unless détente	IIC1 No U.S.S.R. dominance without U.S.S.R. involvement	IID1 No U.S.S.R. dominance without U.S.S.R. involvement
2 Both dominant	IIA2 No U.S. dominance without U.S. involvement	IIB2 No undivided Europe if both involved unless détente	IIC2 No U.S. or U.S.S.R. dominance if neither involved	IID2 No U.S.S.R. dominance without U.S.S.R. involvement
3 Neither dominant	IIA3 No U.S.S.R. relaxation of dominance if U.S. not involved and dominant	IIB3 BUFFER EUROPE	IIC3 RECONSTITUTED EUROPE	IID3 U.S. disengages if no threat from East and Europe not divided
4 U.S. only dominant	IIA4 No U.S. dominance without U.S. involvement	IIB4 No undivided Europe if both involved unless détente	IIC4 No U.S. dominance without U.S. involvement	IID4 LIBERATED E. EUROPE

involved." On this basis alone at least eleven of the thirty-three formal possibilities shown on Chart 1 must be ruled out.[2]

2. The division of Europe would not persist if both superpowers disengaged themselves from or relaxed control over their respective halves of Europe. One must assume that pressures for "normalizing" relations between peoples on opposite sides of the line that had divided Moscow-dominated Europe from the West would prevail if the superpowers were both to "go home" or both were to lose the will to shape the security policies of their respective European allies. This assumption eliminates at least seven more of the thirty-three formal possibilities.[3]

3. As long as each superpower is credibly involved in its half of Europe, Soviet-American détente is a necessary condition for normalizing relations between Eastern Europe and Western Europe. Each superpower possibly may take steps toward decontrol of its European allies to get the other superpower to do the same and thereby create a buffer Europe. Otherwise, and perhaps in any case, the Soviet military presence in Eastern Europe is certain to mean Soviet domination of the security policies of states in that region and therefore a persisting division of Europe. This condition for normalizing relations within Europe appears to rule out three additional possibilities of those shown in Chart 1.[4]

4. Except under the conditions of détente just described, Soviet credible involvement in Eastern Europe means Soviet domination of Eastern Europe. Whereas the United States' military presence in

---

[2] Ruled out are those arrangements which presuppose American withdrawal from Western Europe but specify continued American domination over West European security policies (IA2, IA4, IIA2, IIA4 and IIC4); those which presuppose Soviet withdrawal from Eastern Europe but specify continued Soviet domination of East European security policies (ID1, ID2, IIC1, IID1 and IID2); that which presupposes mutual withdrawal but specifies that the two superpowers maintain their dominant roles in areas from which they have withdrawn (IIC2).

[3] It eliminates those which presuppose that both superpowers disengage, but specify that Europe remains divided (IC1, IC2 and IC4); those which presuppose that both superpowers cease to dominate their respective alliance systems, but specify that Europe remains divided (IA3, IB3 and ID3); and that which assumes disengagement and decontrol by both superpowers (IC3).

[4] It rules out IIB1, IIB2 and IIB4.

and guarantee of the territory of its European allies on a genuine partnership basis does not strain the imagination and has in good part been achieved, a similar Soviet development is highly unlikely, except in the buffer Europe contingency. This asymmetry in the role that the two superpowers play with respect to their respective alliance partners rules out two further possibilities [5] from among the thirty-three and would have ruled out several others if they had not already been eliminated by earlier contradictions.

5. Only a resurrected goal of liberating Eastern Europe (and thus doing away with the division of Europe) would support a continued American military presence in Western Europe if the Soviet Union were to disengage from Eastern Europe. This unlikely circumstance aside, domestic pressures for paring back American deployments in Europe would surely prevail if the Soviet threat to Western Europe were judged to have disappeared. Since withdrawal from Eastern Europe would be the most conclusive evidence of such disappearance, American withdrawal from Western Europe would seem likely to follow, if it had not already preceded, Soviet withdrawal from Eastern Europe. Under the conditions specified, with the resulting perception of abated Soviet threat, two additional possibilities must be eliminated.[6]

There remain, then, as Chart 1 shows, eight types of European security arrangements not demonstrably implausible. The next section delineates the characteristics of these eight models and sketches briefly the paths along which Europe might conceivably move toward one or another of the eight.

II

The ideal type of *Two Spheres Europe* (IB2) closely approximates the real Europe of the early 1970s. In this model, both superpowers are credibly involved. Each has guaranteed the security of its European allies against armed attack by the other superpower or its allies. The formal commitment is buttressed by a scale of preparedness, an extent of military deployment, and a pattern of

[5] They are IB4 and IIA3.   [6] They are ID4 and IID3.

continuing diplomatic action sufficient to make the commitment appear credible to ally and prospective opponent alike. The superpowers remain dominant in their respective alliances.

In the real Europe of the early 1970s, of course, there is an asymmetry; for the superpowers are not equally dominant. The United States is more inclined to consult and be respectful of its allies than is the Soviet Union. This partly may be because of its genuine belief in the sovereign equality of the Atlantic partners, but it is also a reflection of the fact that the major countries of Western Europe remain important powers in their own right, powers of a magnitude which has no counterpart among the non-Soviet Warsaw Pact signatories.

Although Europe in the early 1970s most closely resembles Two Spheres Europe, it exhibits in minor degree characteristics of two other ideal types, and these are models toward which contemporary Europe could quite plausibly move *directly*, as shown in Chart 2.

The first of these types is the *Sheltered Western Europe* model (IB1). In this model, while Moscow continues to exercise firm control over its partners in Eastern Europe and while Washington continues to "keep the nuclear umbrella open" over its NATO allies, who remain very dependent upon the United States for protection, the Western Europeans cut their contributions to Western defense still further below the level that Washington considers their fair share, and United States domination of Atlantic alliance policy becomes much less marked.

Sheltered Western Europe less politely might be called "free-ride" or at least "nuclear free-ride" Western Europe, but the free-ride label has connotations that are not necessarily applicable. Much of the protection the United States provides for its European allies is an unavoidable by-product of protection it is providing for itself; and those in the United States who *prefer* that the United States have a near-monopoly in Western nuclear striking power should not complain about Western Europe's nuclear free ride. In any case, there appears to be a significant margin within which Western European governments could adjust downward their respective shares of the common burden of Western conventional de-

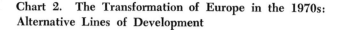

Chart 2.   The Transformation of Europe in the 1970s:
Alternative Lines of Development

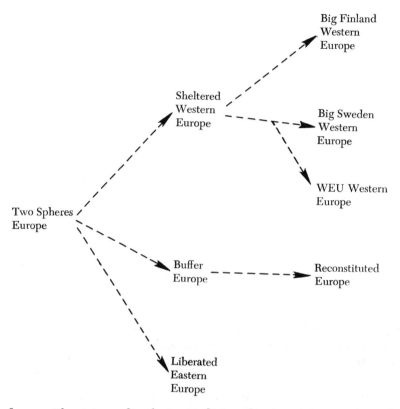

fense without immediately jeopardizing the American guarantee.[7]

The second of these ideal types that appear incipient in the Europe of 1970 is *Buffer Europe* (IIB3). In this arrangement the two superpowers, rejecting the idea of thermonuclear war with each other and rejecting also the use of war to extend their dominant influence into the territory of the present opposing alliance, continue to underwrite the security of their respective allies, but step by step relax the controls they have hitherto exercised. With the terri-

[7] An upward adjustment of the Western European share might, on the other hand, lead ultimately toward *WEU Western Europe* (IA1b on Chart 1, described subsequently).

torial security of Europe in any but a thermonuclear war looking ever more stable and from each superpower's point of view more desirable than any alternative that can be achieved without the risk of thermonuclear war, the superpowers see little point in curbing pressures to normalize relations between Eastern and Western Europe.

There is a third kind of European security arrangement toward which the Europe of the 1970s might possibly move directly: the ideal type designated *Liberated Eastern Europe* (IID4). This is a type often discussed in the days of John Foster Dulles; since the Soviet intervention in Hungary in 1956 and in Czechoslovakia in 1968, it no longer seems plausible. In this model, the Soviet Union withdraws from Eastern Europe altogether. Eastern Europe, whether because of a lack of internal strength to stand as a nonaligned autonomous security system between the Atlantic system and the Soviet Union or because of its basic "Europeanness" and its desire for access to the advanced technology of the West, finds the gravitational pull of Western Europe irresistible. The Europe that lies between the superpowers is no longer divided, and the Atlantic Community expands to include Eastern Europe. For this ideal type to regain plausibility, one would have to posit some catastrophic event which drained Soviet energies away from Eastern Europe, such as a protracted and devastating Sino-Soviet war.

It is difficult to believe that either Sheltered Western Europe or Buffer Europe would be end-points in a transformation of Europe. In the case of Sheltered Western Europe, American preoccupation with urgent domestic concerns, widespread belief that the Soviet threat had greatly lessened, and irritation with European partners perceived as not doing their fair share, especially if developments in military technology made the security of Western Europe seem less relevant to the security of North America, might combine to lead the United States to pare back its contribution to European security and perhaps withdraw altogether.

If it did and if the countries of Western Europe did not move effectively to fill the power vacuum thereby created, the "Finlandization" of Western Europe, to use a word given currency by Pierre

Hassner and Alastair Buchan, might follow promptly.[8] Accordingly, but somewhat inaccurately, a Europe which is no longer divided, but undivided on Soviet terms, is labeled the *Big Finland Western Europe* ideal type (IIA1).[9] With the American nuclear umbrella no longer held over Western Europe that area would be highly susceptible to Soviet pressure and would appear "free" only as long as its behavior met minimum Soviet requirements. Just as Liberated Eastern Europe would be the development least desired by the Soviet Union, Big Finland Western Europe would be the one least desired by the United States.

Suppose, however, that the countries of Western Europe turn out to have the will, the material basis, and the organizational capability to provide for themselves the protection no longer afforded by the United States' nuclear umbrella, presence in Europe, and explicit guarantees. Suppose the Soviet threat does not abate, the hierarchical organization of the Warsaw Treaty Organization countries continues, and Europe remains divided. An autonomous Western Europe, strong enough and united enough to dispense with American military guarantees and stand alone against a Soviet Union still in effective control of Eastern Europe, could emerge. Because security arrangements for this autonomous Western Europe could vary according to the condition of the fourth characteristic, the degree of effective cooperation between North America and Western Europe, there must be two ideal types to represent the case of autonomous Western Europe.

[8] Buchan, *Europe's Futures, Europe's Choices* (New York: Columbia University Press, 1969); and Hassner, *Change and Security in Europe*, Parts I and II, Adelphi Papers Nos. 45 and 49 (London: Institute for Strategic Studies, 1968).

[9] The analogy to Finland is inaccurate and misleading. A Western Europe that neither the Americans nor the Western Europeans had a will to protect is not really very much like the real Finland, whose relations with the Soviet Union necessarily reflect an enormous disparity in size. Finland has less than 2 percent of the population or land area of its great neighbor. Furthermore, Finnish defense policy bears no relation to Western European defense policies, for the modest Finnish goal is hardly more than to prevent a Soviet walkover victory, thus giving Europe and the world a chance to focus on Finland's plight and greatly increasing the political cost to the Soviet Union of a military solution to problems in Soviet-Finnish relations.

If autonomous Western Europe chooses to stand nonaligned, it would, to coin a word by analogy, be "Swedenized." This model is the *Big Sweden Western Europe* version of autonomous Western Europe (IA1a). Suppose, however, that the mood and circumstances attending the American decision to reduce its European commitment or to decommit altogether and the foreign-policy orientations of the political parties then in power in leading European countries were such that the Western European and American governments choose to cooperate effectively with each other. Each is perceived in the eyes of the other as "paying its way," and they face together a strong, tightly organized, and potentially hostile Soviet bloc. This ideal type is the *WEU Western Europe* version of autonomous Western Europe (IA1b). Such a Western European defense community would presumably not be limited to the seven states which currently make up the Western European Union.[10]

Following a second path illustrated in Chart 2, Buffer Europe could well be a way station on the road to a very different kind of Europe, in this case *Reconstituted Europe* (IIC3). In this model, as the Soviet-American détente that would make a Buffer Europe possible continues and perhaps grows more and more stable, barriers would continue to fall between Eastern and Western Europe. As the contingency of war between the superpowers over Europe appears ever more remote, the Soviet Union and the United States more or less symmetrically disengage step by step from their respective systems of military guarantees and credible involvement. Relations between Eastern and Western Europe normalize to the degree that crises in Europe no longer automatically also become

---

[10] Since Eastern Europe, as was noted above, lacks the second-tier powers found in Western Europe and has a security guarantor less disinclined than is Western Europe's to exercise dominance, it does not have the possibility of controlling its own destiny that Western Europe has. Western Europe is imaginable as a viable political entity or autonomous subsystem in world politics; Eastern Europe is not. Since no one can imagine an autonomous Eastern Europe standing strong and self-reliant against both East and West, or one which while protected by the Soviet Union is permitted to take important initiatives of its own in East-West relations, it is proper that there be no analogue in the East to WEU or Big Sweden or Sheltered Western Europe.

crises in Soviet-American relations. With the Europe that lies between the superpowers managing its own crises and with the two superpowers reasonably confident that it is so internally balanced that an undivided Europe could be turned against neither of them, this key area in world politics becomes a genuinely autonomous subsystem in the global system. In this ideal type, Europe ceases to be divided, but on European terms.

III

Two of the eight models are not likely to find counterparts in the real Europe of the 1970s and 1980s, namely, Big Finland Western Europe and Liberated Eastern Europe. As long as the position of the United States and the Soviet Union is that domination of Europe by the other would upset the balance between the superpowers, neither country's leaders will voluntarily tolerate movement toward the set of European security arrangements which would be "worst" for it. Thus it is likely that if the closing American nuclear umbrella seemed to be moving Western Europe in the Big Finland direction, the umbrella would begin to open again. Similarly, the Soviet leaders can be expected to resist movement away from Two Spheres Europe and toward Liberated Eastern Europe.

As the image of the closing and opening umbrella suggests, if either or both superpowers were to disengage militarily from Europe, they would not simply "opt out"—here today, gone tomorrow. The symmetrical relaxation of superpower vigilance which would permit movement along the path from Two Spheres Europe to Buffer Europe and the symmetrical disengagement which would transform Buffer Europe into Reconstituted Europe might very well not occur with great fanfare and by huge steps. Relaxation and disengagement would be subject to reversal if the threat from the other side again seemed to grow.

The same is true of movement along paths leading toward Sheltered Western Europe and WEU Western Europe, as the United States and its NATO allies adjust downward or upward their respective contributions and commitments to joint protection against a Soviet threat. The movement toward these security arrangements, especially at their beginnings, will probably exhibit characteristics of two or more of the eight ideal types. Thus the real Europe of the early 1970s, which with its features of both Sheltered Western Europe and Buffer Europe departs from the ideal-type Two Spheres Europe in significant ways, may not move toward either pure type but toward a mixed type, with the sheltered characteristic more pronounced in Western Europe than in Eastern Europe but present there, too, and with the two parts of Europe together forming a buffer between the superpower guarantors. Similarly, if the American nuclear umbrella over a Sheltered Western Europe were to begin to close, there would be several possible intermediate outcomes between Big Finland and Big Sweden Western Europe and between Big Sweden and WEU Western Europe.

As this discussion of mixed types suggests, the concept of the ideal type does not require that every country in Europe (or in a sphere of Europe) conforms to the security arrangements prescribed for it by a particular model. To say, for example, that Big Sweden Western Europe will be the prevailing ideal type is to say that most of the Western European states (and particularly most of the important ones) will pursue their security objectives somewhat the way Sweden (or Switzerland) currently does. Big Sweden Western Europe will be the *modal* configuration. Each ideal type represents a modal configuration, and movement from one type toward another means a shifting of modalities. The fact that some states may be seeking security in ways not covered by the prevailing model is one of the realities that the model must abstract from in order to be a model, to be of analytical value.

The models, then, are not meant to be close replicas of either present or future worlds. They are also not intended to be prescriptive. None is an end in itself, and except for Big Finland Western Europe, there is no presumption that one is any better suited than another to serve the American interest in the security of Western Europe and peace on the Continent. Moreover, as previously noted, the models themselves provide no direct clues to the political, economic, military, and social developments which could produce one or another of these major security arrangements or to the structure of the international institutions and organizations that might be associated with those developments.

What the models do is to focus attention on the prime characteristics of the major configurations that European security arrangements could take in the next decade and thus make easier the task of assaying the consequences for European security arrangements of the actual trends and developments which will shape the future. How some of the major developments described in Chapters Two and Three might lead to each of these models is discussed in the next chapter.

/ Chapter Five

future security
arrangements: possible
patterns of stability and change

I

THE PREVIOUS CHAPTER described the possible outcomes from changes in European security arrangements and some
of the paths by which Europe might move toward one or another
ideal-type outcome. The defining characteristics of the eight models considered are useful for assaying the potential consequences of
forces making for continuity or change in security arrangements,
but they do not in themselves provide a means of identifying the
forces that may actually make for continuity or change in the
1970s.

Identification of these forces is the task of this chapter.[1] It starts
with an analysis of the circumstances that will have to prevail if the

[1] Parts of this analysis build upon the ideas and insights of many analysts
on both sides of the Atlantic who have invested thought and effort into pro-
jecting Europe into the 1970s. Although it is believed that this analysis goes
somewhat beyond earlier work, the authors nevertheless acknowledge their intellectual debts to Alastair Buchan, *Europe's Futures, Europe's Choices* (New
York: Columbia University Press, 1969); Pierre Hassner, *Change and Security*

1970s are to end as they begin: with European security arrangements approximating the model of Two Spheres Europe. The chapter next examines the prospects for change in some of these circumstances and how these changes could lead Europe toward
other model security arrangements.[2] Finally, an effort is made to
rank the plausibility of these changes and to describe the most immediate shape of the future.

II

If an approximation of Two Spheres Europe is to endure
throughout the 1970s, certain conditions must persist. The United
States must maintain its nuclear commitment, and the credibility of
the commitment must not erode away completely. Maintaining
credibility at a high level requires that Western European leaders
feel sure that Americans consider the security of Western Europe
and of the United States to be so indivisible that if necessary, the
United States will use strategic nuclear weapons in response to a
major Soviet attack, regardless of the devastation such a use would
bring to the American continent, and that the Russians know this.
Factors that bolster credibility are enough United States nuclear
superiority over the Soviets to ensure that in a nuclear exchange
Soviet losses will be much larger than American losses; [3] military

in Europe, Parts I and II, Adelphi Papers Nos. 45 and 49 (London: Institute
for Strategic Studies, 1968); Lincoln P. Bloomfield, *Western Europe to the
Mid-Seventies: Five Scenarios* (Cambridge: Center for International Studies,
Massachusetts Institute of Technology, 1968); Herman Kahn, Edmund Still-
man, and Anthony Wiener, *Alternatives for European Defense in the Next
Decade* (New York: Hudson Institute, 1964); Herman Kahn and William Pfaff,
"Our Alternatives in Europe," *Foreign Affairs*, July, 1965; and Steven War-
necke, "Models for the Future of Western and Eastern Europe," *Studies for a
New Central Europe*, Series 2 (1968/1969).

[2] Techniques of systems analysis applied in generating projected sequences
of events during the 1970s are described in a note on methodology at the end
of this volume.

[3] What is more important here than actual American superiority is the *ap-
pearance* of it. Credibility endures as long as the Russians perceive American
superiority. Or for some of the patterns all that matters is that the Western
European NATO allies perceive American superiority or that the Western Europeans perceive that the Russians perceive American superiority.

strategies that provide a means for meeting limited Soviet attacks (with or without tactical nuclear weapons) without requiring the immediate use of United States strategic nuclear weapons; and enough American forces stationed on the Continent to demonstrate involvement with European concerns and to provide a sufficient hostage to insure a nuclear ransom. The United States must also protect Western European countries against a powerful or provocative Germany; American forces on the Continent help to serve this purpose.

The Soviet Union must continue to oppose loss of control over its sphere of Europe and, as a necessary condition for the continuation of American involvement in its sphere, to act in such a manner that at least some key decision-makers in the West intermittently are reinforced in their belief that there is a Soviet threat. The Soviet Union therefore must maintain a large military force in Central Europe, denounce and occasionally threaten NATO, weather Czechoslovakia-like storms, enforce orthodoxy, nip bridge-builders' fingers, and by and large keep Eastern European governments restrained in their relations with the West and respectfully terrified of Moscow.

The major Western European governments, in addition to retaining their confidence in American guarantees against both the Soviet Union and Germany, must accept a second-tier status within the Western security system and marginal influence within the global system. They must share in NATO defense to an extent that seems adequate to Washington, and they must be unwilling or unable to arm and organize in any way that might amplify the Western European voice or role in Western strategic decision-making.

These, then, are the conditions for the preservation of Two Spheres Europe during the 1970s. Conversely, if Two Spheres Europe is to be supplanted by some other security arrangement, one or more of these conditions must change.

Movement toward another model from one that has persisted through twenty years of tumultuous events will not be easy. The status quo, Two Spheres Europe, has lasted not because it is the most favored arrangement for any of the actors involved—the United States, the Soviet Union, the European countries—but because it is the least unfavorable arrangement for all of them to-gether (i.e., it minimizes total dissatisfaction). Thus any attempt by one actor to get to a more favored arrangement—a status quo plus arrangement—is almost certain to represent a status quo minus situation for another actor. That actor then nullifies the initiating action by taking counteraction or by failing to take a necessary complementary action at a crucial point. One effect of this situation is a built-in tendency for security arrangements to "bounce back" to Two Spheres Europe. Another effect is the providing of opportunities in most of the pathways toward change for the United States to determine or influence the outcome.

Only very compelling initial actions accompanied or followed by attempts to entice or coerce necessary complementary actions by other actors can be expected to move the modal configuration away from Two Spheres Europe. The analysis which follows examines the outcomes from five such actions: the Western Europeans cutting their contributions to Western defense; the United States ceasing to be credibly involved in Western Europe; the Western Europeans undertaking their own defense; the United States and the Soviet Union relaxing control over their spheres of Europe; and the Soviet Union withdrawing from its sphere.

III

Pattern I: The Western Europeans Take a Free Ride

Two of the conditions for the preservation of a Two Spheres Europe are that the Western Europeans continue to bear what Washington considers is their fair share of the Western defense effort and that they continue to accept American leadership in decisions affecting that defense effort, such decisions necessarily covering a wide range of diplomatic and military issues. Paying taxes for a common effort in which one does not have an equal voice can lead to frustrations, and for twenty years it has. The Western Europeans could take an obvious step to relieve their frustrations; this analysis shows where that step could lead.

The Soviets remain involved and dominant in Eastern Europe,

but not highly threatening. The American nuclear umbrella remains over Western Europe, its credibility not seriously eroded. Dulled by more than two decades of successful deterrence by American strategic nuclear forces, assured that West Germany is not a threat, and pressured by "turning inward" demands for reallocation of resources to domestic sectors, Western European leaders cut their countries' defense expenditures. Apologizing to Washington, declaiming Western solidarity, and verbally reaffirming commitments, they, as budget follows budget, let Western European contributions to Western defense dwindle in American eyes to tokens, so that nearly the full weight of that defense seems to rest upon American shoulders. At this point, Western Europeans appear to be consumers of a wholly American-produced security.

The same forces that have produced the decrease in defense expenditures lead to an increase in transatlantic political dissension. The turning-inward phenomenon has moved Western European governments to the left (the power of Socialists and Communists in France and Italy and of the Left wing of the West German Social Democrats and the British Labourites is enhanced), with the result that the political role and voice of anti-NATO and anti-American elements are increased. Critics of the United States become more numerous and more vociferous, foreign policies hammered out in coalition governments come to rest at consensus points further from rather than closer to American positions, and efforts to dissociate and differentiate Western European postures from American ones become more frequent and more deliberate as such efforts bring rewards in East-West and in Third World relations. The Leftist voices are joined by voices from Right-nationalist elements (Gaullists, Straussites), who have long resented American domination of Western security policy. The power of the Center-Atlanticist elements declines.

The United States sees its own defense budgets hiked, its balance-of-payments problems increased, its officials and attentive publics irritated by Western Europe criticism and financial defection, its political dominance in the Western security alliance gone (or greatly lessened). But impressed with the necessity of making certain that Western Europe does not fall within the Soviet sphere of influence, the United States maintains its guarantee, and the Western European countries are able to enjoy something of a free ride in a Sheltered Western Europe.

It is also possible that security arrangements could be transformed in the direction of the Sheltered Western Europe model through Western European attempts to use a drastic cut in their NATO contributions as a lever to get an "equal partnership" in the Atlantic alliance. If the United States grants a greater voice to the Western Europeans to get their contributions back to the former level and recognizes this level as their "equal" share, security arrangements move toward the WEU Western Europe model, as explained in Pattern III below. If the United States refuses to revise the partnership arrangement and the Western Europeans decide to restore contributions to their former level to keep what voice they already have in strategic decision-making, the security arrangement bounces back toward the Two Spheres Europe model. But if the Western European countries meet the American refusal with a "no taxation without representation" response, the security arrangement is transformed into a Sheltered Western Europe configuration.

Since operative forces are likely to affect the countries of Western Europe with varying strengths and chronologies, the 1970s may be a period with no modal-configuration security arrangement. Some countries may be maintaining fidelity to the Two Spheres design while others are operating more in accordance with the Sheltered Western Europe model. Various forms of a mixed-type arrangement are possible: Anglo-American Solidarity and the Continent Adrift; The Washington-Bonn Axis; or Every State (or Subregional Cluster) for Itself.[4]

How plausible is this pattern? Previous analysis has indicated that during the 1970s turning-inward pressures in Western European society are likely to be strong: some Western European governments are likely to move to the left (as has already happened in West Germany); American attitudes will reemphasize rather than downgrade the importance of Europe to United States

[4] For development of the idea of subregional clusters, see Nils Ørvik, "NATO, NAFTA and the Smaller Allies," *Orbis*, Summer, 1968.

security; the Soviet Union will not be viewed by Western Europeans as an increased threat; and West German economic and political development will not turn that country into a menace that a cooperating Britain and France cannot handle. Therefore, movement toward Sheltered Western Europe in the mid-to-late 1970s seems quite plausible.

Working against a movement toward Sheltered Western Europe is the strength of Center elements in European political spectrums, with their long-established habits of cooperation in NATO and other transatlantic institutions and their appreciation that increased freedom of action in diplomacy and in domestic financial and political affairs comes at the expense of their influence on the development of American strategic (and tactical) nuclear policy. To the extent that traditional Center attitudes dominate Western European governments, movement toward Sheltered Western Europe is less likely and less extreme.

One point should be stressed: whether movement to or toward Sheltered Western Europe occurs is not really within the American range of choice. The options lie with the Western Europeans (and to some extent the Russians). Once Western European governments have opted for the free ride, there is very little the United States can do to move them back to the Two Spheres Europe model. The only step available to the United States, withdrawal of the American nuclear guarantee, would indeed move governments away from Sheltered Western Europe but toward other models, as the next section demonstrates.[5]

Pattern II: The American Nuclear Umbrella Folds

The reliability of the American nuclear guarantee to Western Europe has been eroding for years, as the Soviet Union's growing second-strike capability has increased the damage that would be

---

[5] The possible dynamics of an American-Western European threat-counter-threat interaction concerning the withdrawal of the American nuclear guarantee are developed more fully in Donald J. Puchala, "NATO and the Future of Europe," *NATO: Prospects for the Seventies* (St. Louis: University of Missouri Center for International Studies, 1970).

done to American lives and property in a nuclear exchange. Western European leaders have preferred not to dwell on this erosion because their only alternative to belief in the reliability of the American nuclear umbrella is expensive self-defense or reliance on Soviet good intentions. It is possible, however, that events in the 1970s might bring to the fore latent doubts about reliability.

One event which could provoke a "credibility crisis" is the recognition of "parity" between American and Soviet strategic nuclear forces, either through a formal arms control agreement or through Soviet claims that are uncontested or admitted by American officials or for other reasons believed by Western European decision-makers. Although the nuclear superiority possessed by the United States for some time has not been sufficient to limit Soviet damage to a magnitude close to that of World War II, the explicit establishment of parity might destroy any illusions about superiority that had existed in Western European minds. Knowledge that the Russians were constructing a heavy ABM system would heighten the effect, and attainment by the Russians of demonstrable superiority would probably blow the umbrella right out of the sky. Even prolonged contemplation of the already adopted strategy for the defense of Europe of slow escalation to nuclear attack (after a conventional-warfare phase) could weaken belief. Because credibility is in the mind of the believer, any event—an action by the Russians that makes them seem more threatening or withdrawal of American troops from Europe—which focuses attention on Western Europe's basic security problems could lead to a loss of faith in the American guarantee.

The Western Europeans' response to loss of belief in the reliability of the American nuclear umbrella could cause movement toward any of three different security models. Heading for WEU Western Europe, the Western Europeans could choose to "prop up" the American deterrent. Forming a nuclear European Defense Community that would manufacture European missiles to supplement the American supply would not be necessary or even helpful. With the advent of MIRVs the United States will need not more warheads but a means of coping with the Soviet warheads it cannot destroy because they have been launched on warning or from submarines. The Western Europeans most practically restore credibility to their ally's deterrent by building antisubmarine-warfare forces and by assuming the whole burden of Western European conventional-warfare defense, thereby freeing American funds and resources for construction of heavy ABM defenses around American cities. The price for the Western Europeans' paying their own way is equal partnership with the United States in strategic decision-making and East-West crisis control. And thus the security arrangement ceases to approximate that of Two Spheres Europe and resembles that of WEU Western Europe.

The Western European choice to move toward the WEU Western Europe model, with its independent but cooperating security forces, would not be likely if loss of credibility occurred while anti-American elements were dominating Western European governments or if the loss occurred in such a way (e.g., through an arms control agreement) as to suggest lack of American concern with Western Europe's fate. In these circumstances the Western Europeans move to Big Sweden Western Europe, that is, they become nonaligned and armed, conventionally or with nuclear weapons, to whatever extent their leaders consider necessary to make the cost of overrunning them prohibitively high for the Russians.

Attainment of either form of autonomous Western Europe requires on the part of the Western Europeans willingness, ability, and time to build their defense forces. If any of these are lacking, the Western Europeans would probably be driven toward a Big Finland Western European security arrangement. They not only dissociate themselves politically and strategically from the United States, as in the Big Sweden Western Europe model, but they also make overtures to the Soviet Union for a settlement and a new modus vivendi. Differences between Western European and Eastern European countries in political, economic, and military autonomy become less and less marked, and Europe ceases to be divided.

The foregoing discussion has dealt with the Western Europeans' responses to their loss of belief in the reliability of the American nuclear umbrella. But the umbrella also might fold because, while still credible, it is deliberately and intentionally withdrawn by the

United States, as turning-inward pressures cause Western Europe to be defined as outside the United States' security sphere. Alternatively, European security arrangements having taken the form of Sheltered Western Europe, American irritation with the Western Europeans' renouncing a fair share of the defense burden and voicing unwelcome political attitudes overbalances American attitudes about the indivisibility of United States' and Western European security.

In this case as in the case of credibility eroding, whether Western Europe moves toward Big Finland Western Europe or toward a version of autonomous Western Europe depends on its willingness, ability, and time for arming for its own defense. There is an important difference, however. The umbrella having been closed voluntarily, with its credibility still intact, it can be opened again. As noted in the previous chapter, movement toward Big Finland Western Europe may cause it to do just that, with the probable result that Western Europe bounces back toward Two Spheres Europe or Sheltered Western Europe.

Between the two versions of autonomous Western Europe, the Western Europeans are not likely to move toward a "pure" form of either. Since the initiating action, the withdrawal of the American nuclear guarantee, removes one important basis for cooperation with the United States, that action in the absence of countervailing pressures would move Western Europe in the Big Sweden rather than in the WEU direction.

With the variety of options open to Western European countries after the closing-up of the American nuclear umbrella, absence of a modal-configuration security arrangement is very probable. Some countries might join together in a WEU arrangement, some might try the Big Sweden pattern and others the Big Finland design, and still others might project ambiguity.

How plausible are any of these movements? With respect to those caused by loss of faith in the credibility of the American commitment, it should be stressed again that most Western Europeans, especially those of the Center, want to keep that faith because of the unpleasantness of the alternatives. (For Leftist or

Right-nationalist elements, the alternatives may be more attractive.)

After all, minor credibility crises have occurred intermittently throughout the last twenty years. Western Europeans have wondered about the geographic scope of the umbrella, e.g., would the United States really initiate a nuclear attack against the Soviet Union if the latter were to move a division or two into the remote northern areas of Norway? Western Europeans have argued with the Americans about how soon, in what number, and on what targets American strategic nuclear weapons and NATO tactical nuclear weapons are to be used, who is to manufacture them, and who is to decide the above questions about their use. Singly and cumulatively these problems have raised Western European suspicions about the American willingness to back up nuclear promises. These perspectives were, of course, most clearly reflected in de Gaulle's decisions to withdraw from NATO and to build the *force de frappe*.

The United States has monitored Western European fears and doubts and responded to them by guaranteeing continued physical presence, by placing under the nuclear umbrella areas and contingencies that Europeans feared had been left out, and by creating enough committees and study groups to give Western European leaders a sense of enhanced roles in strategic decision-making. Enough belief in American guarantees has been restored to the minds of most Western European leaders to make the modal-configuration security arrangement bounce back to its approximation of the Two Spheres Europe model.

Working to help Western Europeans keep their faith in the reliability of the American guarantee throughout the 1970s are several developments mentioned in previous chapters. The widened absolute gap between American and Soviet gross national products expected by the end of the decade and domestic pressures limiting Soviet utilization or resources for military purposes will make achievement of a dramatically decisive and obvious Soviet superiority in nuclear weapons difficult. The immediate effect of the introduction of MIRV and ABM technologies will be to increase the credibility of the American deterrent, and the ultimate effect will be to allow both superpowers to claim superiority. The upgrading of American concern with Europe relative to that shown for other parts of the world will help make Western Europeans feel that their problems are getting the attention they merit.

The developments which could most certainly shake the credibility of the American guarantee are actions taken by the Soviet Union that are perceived by the Western Europeans as increasing the threat from that quarter, technological innovations that allow the Russians to achieve decisive, demonstrable superiority in nuclear weapons, and reduction of the number of American troops on the Continent. The first development is not subject to American control and the second only partly so, but the effects of the third development on credibility could certainly be mitigated by the United States' prefacing and accompanying withdrawals with explanations and reaffirmations of commitment.

An arms control agreement between the United States and the Soviet Union establishing parity in nuclear forces, which is partly within American control, could work in either direction. Certification of the end of American superiority could weaken credibility, but agreement by the Russians to end or limit the arms race could make them seem less threatening and thus strengthen confidence in existing security arrangements.

The plausibility of American withdrawal of the nuclear commitment during the 1970s depends on the relative strengths of, on the one hand, transatlantic feelings of solidarity; American appreciation of the negative effect of withdrawal on Soviet and Third World minds; American concern with the costs of losing the Western European resource base; and on the other hand, desire for Soviet-American détente; realization, crystallized by contemplation of MIRVs and ABMs, that denial of the European resource base to a potential aggressor has long ceased to have the importance for American security that it once had; desire to escape the extra costs that maintaining superiority entails; and if Western security has become arranged according to the sheltered Western Europe model, American irritation with what is regarded as too small a

European contribution to the common defense and too much political deviation.

The test of time—almost twenty-five years of it—has shown how strong the former factors are. It would therefore take an extraordinary increase in Soviet-American détente to provoke even a minor reconsideration of or relaxation in the American nuclear commitment. In the same way it would take extreme and prolonged episodes in Western European political deviation to provoke American reconsideration of the commitment and profound attitude changes in the United States to cause a Europe-excluded, neo-isolationist redefinition of national security. No doubt there are European actions that would lead to a withdrawal of the American commitment. Should the Western European governments, for example, proclaim their neutrality as the United States was engaged in an at-the-brink confrontation with the Soviet Union or China in some non-European part of the world, Americans might well feel a sense of betrayal that would lead them to question the whole basis of the American involvement in Europe. But in any less extreme case withdrawal of the commitment would risk costs that are perceived to be too high for rewards that are of uncertain worth and in any event remote.

If the American nuclear umbrella should fold up for any reason, whether Western European countries move toward Big Finland or autonomous Western Europe depends, as has been said, on whether they have the willingness, ability, and time to arm. As noted previously, the Western European countries as a whole have now and will have throughout the 1970s the population and the economic and technological capacity to produce all the conventional-warfare forces needed for self-defense. Britain and France also have some nuclear capability, but providing the necessary tactical and strategic weapons for an independent deterrent for Western Europe would require an extended and joint effort.

Does the basis exist for that extended and joint effort? The Western Europeans have not demonstrated any strong desires to increase defense expenditures, and turning-inward manifestations can be expected to decrease rather than increase inclinations to spend money on arms. Moreover, providing all of their own conventional-warfare forces would require some degree of military and political integration; and as previously pointed out, providing their own strategic nuclear deterrent would require time and considerable further military, political, and economic integration, areas where the Western Europeans do not now seem inclined to make much rapid progress.

The shock of losing the American nuclear umbrella, however, could provide the impetus for a change in attitudes about the desirability of increasing defense expenditures and pursuing wider and deeper integration. The Western Europeans might believe that conventional forces would be sufficient to protect them because of a cooperative arrangement that exchanged Western European contributions to Western defense for some protection by a still credible American nuclear umbrella or because of a gamble that however neutral they were, in a confrontation with the Russians some form of the American umbrella would be covering them or because they were confident that the Russians would not use nuclear weapons against them. On the basis of a conventional-weapons defense system, the Western Europeans could achieve a WEU or Big Sweden Western Europe security arrangement during the 1970s. If they believed that their autonomy required instead or in addition the possession of an independent force of tactical and strategic nuclear weapons, they could not reach either type of autonomous Western Europe in the 1970s, but could be well on their way toward it.

Whether the Western Europeans, having decided to arm for self-defense, chose transatlantic cooperation or nonalignment probably would depend mainly on their calculations of how much certain and useful protection from American nuclear power could be purchased with their contributions to the common defense or obversely, what the chances of and need for American protection were likely to be, these being clearly affected by their estimates of the Soviet threat. All calculations would be affected by the relative strengths in the political arenas of Center compared to Left and Right-nationalist elements, just as basic decisions concerning how much to arm or what kind of settlement to seek with the Soviet

Union would be greatly influenced by the extent to which Right elements were prevailing over the Left.

In the sequence of events surrounding the closing of the American umbrella each of the main actors in the cast—Americans, Western Europeans, Russians—can initiate the action, as can also a "force," namely, technological development. The United States' range of choice includes actions to maintain or withdraw the umbrella and subject to considerable limitations, actions to preserve its credibility. To that extent it can control movements away from Two Spheres Europe. Once credibility is destroyed, however, the United States can do little to prevent movement away from Two Spheres Europe and little to influence whether the outcome is Big Finland Western Europe or a version of autonomous Western Europe; that choice is mainly up to the Western Europeans. If they opt for self-defense and autonomy, the United States can influence their further choice between WEU and Big Sweden Western Europe. The Russians by their actions and responses with respect to arms races, proposals for global and local détente, and control of their sphere of Europe can significantly affect the sequence of events throughout.

Pattern III: The Western Europeans Buy Their Own Umbrella (or at Least a Raincoat)

One of the conditions for maintaining a Two Spheres Europe type of European security arrangement is that the Western Europeans remain satisfied with being contributing but secondary partners in the Atlantic alliance and second-tier powers in global affairs. This status, as has been pointed out, can cause frustrations. The Western Europeans might try to relieve these frustrations not by cutting their contributions, as in Pattern I, but by increasing them and demanding an "equal partnership" with the United States. Such an attempt could cause movement from Two Spheres Europe toward WEU or Big Sweden Western Europe even under conditions of high American commitment and credibility.

Suppose that under such conditions and with the Russians' provocations routine and therefore their threat level low Western Europeans become politically restive and turn their external priorities and attentions toward enhancing their political status and influence. Because Center-Right, Right-Center, or Right governments are in power, the Western Europeans seek their external political fortunes by pushing for truly functional United States–European equality in strategic decision-making and East-West crisis control —and the further Right their orientation, the harder they push.[6]

The lever for prying open access to American decision-making or for getting a European finger on the nuclear trigger is Western European armament. By reversing trends of proportionally decreasing defense expenditures and revitalizing the European Defense Community design (probably in modified form to avoid a replay of the 1950–1954 debate), a Western European Defense Community achieves a capability that may not provide an independent strategic deterrent but permits the Western Europeans to take such a variety of nuclear initiatives that the coordination of American and Western European nuclear-weapons command-and-control decisions becomes critical.

The attainment of capability is followed by a Western European bid for equal partnership, formalized perhaps in a restructured NATO. At this point the United States says either yes or no. An affirmative American answer suggests Washington's reasoning to the conclusion that Western Europe remains vital to American security and that coordination on an equal partnership basis is preferable to alternatives under which Western European behavior could be less predictable and less amenable to American influence.

With the establishment of the revised partnership agreement Western Europe moves away from Two Spheres Europe toward WEU Western Europe. Whether the outcome is actually WEU Western Europe or some intermediate type between it and Two Spheres Europe depends on the extent to which the Western Euro-

---

[6] American and Western European (i.e., French, West German, British, and Italian) interests in non-European areas and issues are by no means wholly congruent. Transatlantic differences concerning the Near East, Africa, and Asia could sharpen in the future, as the myth of Atlantic community loses meaning and adherents.

pean nuclear capability represents in the eyes of the Americans a genuinely equal sharing of the burdens of Western defense and the extent to which the Western Europeans exercise a truly equal voice in alliance decision-making, the second almost certainly being related to the first.

If the United States turns down the request for a revised partnership agreement, the Western Europeans, especially if their nuclear armament is far short of that necessary to constitute an independent deterrent, may feel disgruntled but accept the decision (perhaps vowing to raise the question again after they have achieved more nuclear capability), and the security arrangement bounces back to the Two Spheres Europe model.

On the other hand, if the Western Europeans already have at the time of the negative answer considerable nuclear capability and if they are optimistic about the chances of the United States' in any event providing the rest of the umbrella should rain seriously threaten or about the chances of the climate permanently drying up, they may move toward Big Sweden Western Europe. They sever ties with NATO, adopt foreign policies which reflect neutralist themes, and perhaps even make overtures to the Soviet Union for local détente and a European settlement much more in accord with Russian preferences than any now conceivable.

If the United States responds to Western Europe's request for equal partnership by withdrawing the nuclear commitment, thus challenging Western Europe to go it alone, the movement away from the Two Spheres Europe model might be rapid and perhaps even abrupt. Unless the crisis in European-American relations comes only after Western Europe's rearmament is far advanced, the resulting Big Sweden type of Western Europe might be very short-lived and dependent on a gamble that the United States in an extreme crisis would reopen the nuclear umbrella. To lose that gamble almost inevitably would mean that it was the Big Finland model toward which Western Europe had actually moved—a result that Americans, Western Europeans, and Russians can hardly fail to foresee.

Western Europe's bid for equal partnership could be pursued somewhat less spectacularly than by nuclear blackmail. As in the prop-up operations of Pattern II, the Western Europeans take over responsibility for performing certain of the tasks of the Western defense effort (e.g., antisubmarine warfare, European conventional warfare). They do this gradually, by installments, and *pari passu* earn equality in the Atlantic alliance. The United States might actively encourage these efforts, especially if turning-inward pressures for reduced defense expenditures had become very strong or if it was much involved in a non-European part of the world, fending off Chinese thrusts at American interests in the Far East, for example.

It is also conceivable that the Western Europeans might take an exactly opposite course, that is, attempt to get equal partnership in the alliance by cutting or threatening to cut their contributions. An American refusal to modify the terms of the transatlantic partnership causes the arrangement to bounce back to Two Spheres Europe or move to Sheltered Western Europe, as explained in the analysis of Pattern I. If the United States decides that contributions restored to all or most of the former amount are worth a revised partnership agreement, the closer to an "equal" share it chooses to consider this restored amount and the more voice it gives Western Europeans in alliance decisions, the closer to the WEU Western Europe model the security arrangement moves on its path from Two Spheres Europe. Thus it is possible, although not at all probable, that the Western Europeans might achieve a WEU Western Europe type of security arrangement without any increased expenditures for defense or with even slight decreases.

As in the preceding scenarios, the plausibility of these pathways to WEU and Big Sweden Western Europe depends mainly on the plausibility of the initiating step. To Britons, Frenchmen, and Germans who can remember the days when their countries dominated not only Europe but much of the rest of the world, second-class status and limited influence must be exasperating and not compensated for by involvement in regional concerns and enterprises. Nonetheless, most Western Europeans agree that less-than-equal transatlantic cooperation has yielded enormous rewards; by means of it military security has come to Western Europe (except for Britain perhaps) cheaply enough to permit huge investments in public and private sectors not related to security.

And now with turning-inward pressures exerting their influence expenditures for security are more likely to be cut than increased. Then, too, the Common Market notwithstanding, some of the momentum has been drained from the European unity movement during the past ten years, and new sensitivities about national status and sovereignty have emerged within Europe.[7] In short, the time when Western European defense could have been regionally integrated has probably passed and new opportunities for such integration are not likely to arise until the 1980s or 1990s.

With the American commitment firm and credible and the Soviet threat low (with the result that access to American strategic and crisis decision-making is less urgent), a more dynamic force than a shift of political power to the right would be required to make the Western Europeans decide to arm. The only precipitating force now imaginable is an outburst of scientific and technological activity that produces rapid growth rates and enhanced feelings of competence and self-sufficiency. The chances of this occurring are not great.

Moreover, if nuclear weapons are part of the Western European arms program, even a powerful impulse to rearm would be impeded by feelings about the Germans. Few non-Germans would be unconcerned about a German finger on—or even near—a nuclear trigger, but a regional nuclear force without West German participation is improbable. What would be a better way to weld a Washington-Bonn axis or stimulate nuclear development in Germany than to exclude the Federal Republic from a regional defense arrangement? Many Western Europeans would choose no nuclear force in place of a nuclear force with German participation.

[7] For assessments of the prospect for more comprehensive European integration, see Karl W. Deutsch et al., *France, Germany and the Western Alliance: A Study of Elite Attitudes on European Integration and World Politics* (New York: Charles Scribner's Sons, 1967). See also Puchala, "NATO and the Future of Europe." For some contrasting views, see Ronald Inglehart, "An End to European Integration?" *American Political Science Review*, March, 1967, pp. 91–106; Leon N. Lindberg, "The European Community as a Political System: Notes Toward the Construction of a Model," *Journal of Common Market Studies*, March, 1967, pp. 344–87; Ernst B. Haas, "The Uniting of Europe and the Uniting of Latin America," *Journal of Common Market Studies*, March, 1967, pp. 315–43.

Western Europe's arming for political clout would be subject to the same economic and technological limitations as arming because of the disappearance of the American nuclear umbrella. Conventional forces could be produced with current capabilities and a fairly small amount of military and political integration. So, probably, could minimal nuclear forces, but the closer these forces approach a full independent strategic deterrent the more would new technological capacity and political, military, and economic integration be required, and thus the less likely it is that one or the other version of autonomous Western Europe could be reached during the 1970s.

Similarly, the success of the nuclear EDC in forcing truly equal partnership within the Atlantic alliance would seem to depend mainly on the degree to which the EDC provided a genuinely independent deterrent, unless domestic or other-parts-of-the-world pressures had become so intense that the United States was willing to make concessions to get any kind of help with its security burdens. This prospect is not very likely at present.

In this sequence of events, as in the one involving Sheltered Western Europe, it is the Western Europeans who must start the action. Americans cannot do much to begin the movement to autonomous Western Europe, but once the Western Europeans are on the way, the United States can by its choices influence whether WEU or Big Sweden Western Europe is the final outcome or whether the security arrangement bounces back toward the present Two Spheres model. The Russians sit in the wings and by the provocativeness or quietness or seductiveness of their behavior also affect pathways and outcomes.

Pattern IV: The United States and the Soviet Union End the Cold War in Europe

In this pattern the Russians come out of the wings and join the Americans in center front while the Western Europeans move to the back of the stage. Together these actions symbolize Europe's current status: within the global international system, a subsystem whose fate in the 1970s could mainly be determined by decisions made in Washington and Moscow. Crudely stated, Europe remains an object of American-Soviet politics; and regardless of European preferences, decisions by the superpowers in the 1970s could render the region a wasteland, a battlefield, an arena of continuing Cold War tension, or conceivably a neutralized buffer zone set between global contenders.[8]

This last alternative would be the outcome of an understanding between the superpowers in which each rejects war as a means of extending its influence into the European sphere of the other and consequently relaxes the controls it has hitherto exercised in its sphere but continues to guarantee the security of its sphere against any outsider, including the other.

This understanding could result from one of several events. After an at-the-brink confrontation over a European issue had narrowly missed turning into a nuclear war, each superpower might conclude that augmentation of its influence in the other's sphere was not worth the risk of war.[9] Or contemplation of the MIRV technology, with its increased strain toward preemptive action, might cause American and Soviet leaders and other elites to decide that steps must be taken to keep the possibilities for confrontation at an absolute minimum. Or the understanding could be merely one phase of a general, global Soviet-American détente.

In implementing the understanding, the United States and the Soviet Union exchange dismantlement of NATO for dismantlement of the Warsaw Treaty Organization, removal of the American military presence from Western Europe for removal of the Soviet military presence from Eastern Europe, and abandonment of special American commitments to West Germany for abandonment of special Russian commitments to East Germany. Mutual acceptance by the superpowers of each European state's political-ideological free-

---

[8] International political hierarchy with superpower control is the thrust and essence of Raymond Aron's analysis of contemporary international politics. See *Peace and War* (New York: Doubleday & Company, 1966), pp. 71–93.

[9] Numerous observers and analysts believe that significant learning experiences resulted from the Cuban missile crisis of 1962. Moscow and Washington each recognized the lurking imminence of nuclear war and the great disproportion between possible political gains from penetrating the adversary's spheres and probable human and material costs of nuclear war.

dom of choice, mutual renunciations of interference in the affairs of European states, and some form of defense guarantee to Europe then formally terminate the regional Cold War contest. European governments perhaps are asked to exchange disarmament commitments for an end to the division of the Continent and neutrality pledges for superpower guarantees against interference in regional affairs. The outcome is Buffer Europe, with a zone of superpower disinterestedness between the Atlantic and the Soviet frontier, an undivided Europe rendered militarily secure by joint superpower commitment and harmless by military self-denial.[10]

Of course the movement to Buffer Europe would probably not proceed as rapidly as implied here. A more realistic picture is one in which the United States, the Soviet Union, and European governments grope toward a design for gradual superpower disengagement across a widening neutral zone (probably, although not necessarily, growing eastward and westward from Central European starting points). Within this zone, shifts in the political postures of European states from alliance to neutrality coincide with denuclearization and other local disarmament procedures, with successive severings of formal ties to respective superpowers, and perhaps with successive inductions into new all-European international organizations.

How likely is it that the superpowers would agree to bufferize Europe? Respective disengagements from political-military control in Eastern and Western Europe, abandonment of WTO and NATO defense mechanisms, neutralization from the Atlantic to the Soviet frontier, and dramatic, uncertain departures from established habits of cold warfare in Europe are not among American or Russian first choices for a European security arrangement in the 1970s. As a

---

[10] As bizarre as the Buffer Europe outcome may sound at present, it should be noted that this system is a logical result of the many, varied schemes of East-West disengagement proposed and debated and rejected, but at least seriously studied, in the middle and late 1950s. It is not inconceivable that a new political context of Soviet-American détente might resurrect buffer designs. See Charles R. Planck, *Sicherheit in Europa* (Munich: R. Oldenbourg Verlag, 1968); Bruce M. Russett and Carolyn Cooper, "Major Proposals for Arms Control in Europe: A Review," Appendix 3 to *Arms Control in the European Political Environment* (Final Report to the U.S. Arms Control and Disarmament Agency, Yale University Political Science Research Library, 1966).

first choice each superpower would probably prefer a deterioration of its adversary's position in Europe matched by an improvement in its own. Moreover, neutralization may not be among the superpowers' second choices for the 1970s, because the status quo, no matter how unsatisfactory, could well be preferred to the dissolution of alliances—Soviet proposals to this end notwithstanding.[11]

Consequently, as long as the superpowers continue to perceive opportunities for diplomatic or strategic gains from contests in and about Europe or as long as they can preserve the stalemated status quo on the divided continent, major initiatives toward bufferization are unlikely. The systematic change implied in bufferization is too dramatic to be prompted by any but momentous events. The events would have to be really momentous; the tension generated by the confrontation mentioned above would have to be considerably greater than any so far generated in the Berlin crises, or the degree of détente would have to be considerably greater than any American-Soviet thaw so far experienced. In short, there may be no conditions that could scare or entice the superpowers away from competition in Europe.

Moreover, should a Buffer Europe security arrangement emerge, its life probably must be short. As the prospect of war grows more remote, as the division between the two spheres disappears, relations among the countries of Europe are no longer channeled by the exigencies of the Cold War. Countries in Western Europe form political, economic, and cultural connections with countries in Eastern Europe, and Europe comes to look somewhat like the Europe of the 1920s—a Europe from which America and Russia, for very different reasons, had retreated. It is able to effect a balance against a reunited and resurgent Germany. This Europe is capable of managing its own crises; they no longer automatically become crises in Soviet-American relations. The superpowers feel able to withdraw their guarantees, and Reconstituted Europe becomes a genuinely autonomous subsystem in the global system.

[11] Soviet proposals for a European security conference have called for the dissolution of NATO and WTO as one outcome normalizing intra-European relations. See Marshall D. Shulman, "Soviet Proposals for a European Security Conference," *Arms Control and European Security in the 1970s; Background Papers* (ACDA / IR-152).

One can imagine, although not in the 1970s, an alternative version of noncontrolled, nonguaranteed, nondivided, autonomous Europe, namely, a united Europe with pooled resources and military power of a kind and quantity sufficient to make it a third superpower. It could be called Third Force Europe. Among the ways it might come about are by an autonomous Western Europe (WEU or Big Sweden Western Europe) drawing the Eastern European countries into its sphere of influence, as will be explained in the discussion of Pattern V, or through the countries of Reconstituted Europe forming a Grand Alliance against a particular intra-European threat.

The United States and the Soviet Union together are initiators of the two precipitating events of Pattern IV: the relaxation of controls that transforms Two Spheres Europe into Buffer Europe and the withdrawal of guarantees that transforms Buffer Europe into Reconstituted Europe. Each superpower can act only in concert (although perhaps alternating concert) with the other. Western Europe, as noted at the beginning of the sequence, is very definitely backstage during the decision-making.

It should be mentioned that Buffer Europe is not the only or even the most likely European security arrangement that could result from *global* détente between the United States and the Soviet Union. Buffer Europe might be the European species of several neutral zones set up by a settlement that ended the Cold War. But such a settlement could provide for other arrangements. It could divide the world into clearly defined spheres, with relations between the spheres in the hands of Washington and Moscow. The resulting European security arrangement would be a very rigid Two Spheres Europe. Or the settlement could recognize the emergence of a situation in which the feuds and quarrels of the mid-twentieth century were superseded by new contests in a late-twentieth century multipolar world and in which the United States and the Soviet Union found themselves as often allied as at odds. In this world Europe's security arrangement presumably would take the form of Reconstituted Europe. Or the settlement might provide for global condominium, with the United States and the Soviet Union actively collaborating to police and thereby effectively control the world. Condominium would presumably result in a security arrangement for Europe similar to that proclaimed for Germany at the close of World War II. The prospect of Soviet-American détente on a global basis during the 1970s is so slight that assessing the relative plausibilities of these settlements is difficult and unprofitable.

Buffer Europe, Two Spheres Europe, and Condominium Europe security arrangements leave Europe dependent on the superpowers for security from intra-European disputes and outsiders' attacks. Only in the case of Reconstituted Europe is Europe responsible for its own internal and external security. To put it another way, Reconstituted Europe is the only one of the eight models in which no European country is dependent on a superpower for security.

Pattern V: The Soviet Union Disappears from Eastern Europe

Almost as remote as the possibility of global détente between the superpowers is the possibility that Soviet control and guarantees disappear from Eastern Europe while the United States maintains its involvement and leadership in Western Europe. Nevertheless, several conceivable events could produce a Soviet disappearance. A protracted and devastating Chinese-Soviet war might drain energies away from Eastern Europe. Or Eastern Europe might become such a costly liability for Moscow that the Soviets decide to withdraw. Or bridge-building, despite Soviet objections, might succeed in establishing irreversible interdependence among Eastern and Western European countries, while the same kinds of ambiguities about commitment in peripheral areas that plague American credibility hamper Soviet credibility.

What could conceivably emerge from this last cause is a series of gradual Eastern European reorientations westward, culminating in short dashes to the protection of Western nuclear umbrellas. Even though no one of these movements seems sufficiently provocative to cause Moscow to launch World War III, their sum, permitted to accumulate, amounts to Soviet ejection from some or all of Eastern Europe.

Soviet withdrawal or Eastern European defection erases the dividing line in Europe. The power vacuum in Eastern Europe is filled by American involvement and commitment, and a Liberated Eastern Europe or partially Liberated Eastern Europe arrangement emerges. If at the time the Soviets disappear from Eastern Europe the Western European security arrangement has taken the form of WEU or Big Sweden Western Europe, Western Europe might itself guarantee the security of the Eastern European countries. In that case, what emerges is a form of the Third Force Europe security arrangement described in the analysis of Pattern IV.

The plausibility of these pathways from Two Spheres Europe to Liberated Eastern Europe or from autonomous Western Europe to Third Force Europe turns mainly on the likelihood of Soviet disappearance from Eastern Europe. Nothing in recent history—the Czechoslovak situation, the Brezhnev Doctrine, the power of orthodox Soviet elites—suggests that the Soviet Union will in the next decade be prepared to let the Eastern European countries escape from its sphere of influence into that of the United States or the Western European countries. At the same time, little evidence suggests that Eastern Europeans are eager or even willing to jump from one sphere of influence into another. To say that Eastern European elites prefer to move *away* from Soviet influence does not imply that they would prefer to move politically, socially, or culturally *toward* the West. Hence, only some event as catastrophic as the Chinese-Soviet war mentioned above could compel the Soviet Union to release Eastern Europe, and even this release might not end the division of Europe.

In this sequence the initiating action for withdrawal must, of course, come from the Soviet Union. In the escape of the Eastern European countries to the West, the Eastern European countries, the Western European countries, and the United States all play a role, but an effective one, probably, only if the Soviet Union's attention is focused somewhere else in the world.

IV

The most immediately plausible future is, of course, the present. Limited movement away from the Two Spheres Europe system, reactions by actors for whom the movement is a status quo minus step, and return to the Two Spheres arrangement is the most probable course of events in the European security arena for the next several years.

The United States, as it has in recent years, will try to make its nuclear umbrella over Europe credible to itself, the Western Europeans, and the Russians. It will continue to ask the Western Europeans to assume a greater share of the defense burden. The Russians, aware that the Two Spheres Europe arrangement at least secures for them two traditional objectives of Russian foreign policy, an Eastern European defense glacis and a controlled Germany, will try to entice the West into a formal recognition of the division of Europe, of Soviet suzerainty over its half, and of the legitimacy of the German Democratic Republic.

The Western Europeans will criticize American rashness while questioning American cautiousness, will encourage East-West détente while fearing Soviet-American condominium, and will earnestly debate American political and strategic decisions after they have been made and are irreversible. In actions, however, Western harmony will prevail, at least in security matters and in questions concerning East-West relations. Their lack of good options and the arrangement's value in controlling Germany will keep the Western Europeans from disrupting the Two Spheres Europe arrangement.

But as the decade progresses, there is less certainty that the Two Spheres arrangement will persist. As possible patterns discussed here have illustrated, there are events which could move Europe toward a different security arrangement. Insofar as the initiating events that provided the starting points for the various sequences are concerned, the discussion showed that their plausibility can be ranked in the order in which they were presented: a reduction in Western European expenditures for defense; a folding or blowing away of the American umbrella; a movement toward Western European self-defense; a Soviet-American move to end the division of Europe; and a Soviet withdrawal from Eastern Europe. Accordingly, the outcomes that followed these events can also be ranked, although somewhat more tentatively.

The plausibilities, feasibilities, and probabilities that can be attached to the different patterns suggest (using Chart 2 in Chapter

Four as a guide) that movement from Two Spheres Europe more likely will be toward Sheltered Western Europe than toward Buffer Europe, and that if there is movement from Sheltered Western Europe, it is more likely to be toward autonomous Western Europe than toward Big Finland Western Europe (provided—and it is a key point—that erosion of the American commitment has been more the result of American disengagement than of Western European disbelief). If autonomous Western Europe is the outcome, Big Sweden is a more likely version than WEU Western Europe.

Although the analysis suggests these conclusions, its purpose has been not to predict the future but to identify the manner in which the present might change. Above all, its purpose has been to show that the future is not a book that once opened can be confidently closed. The point in delineating the changes that *could* occur has been to identify the issues and choices through which the United States may influence the direction and content of the future that will occur.

two spheres europe's future and the limits of american choice

I

TRENDS, MODELS, AND SCENARIOS are important in this analysis of future European security arrangements only as they clarify choices in American policy relating to arms and arms control. The concluding two chapters deal with those choices. This chapter describes the range and imperatives of American choice and argues that choosing Western Europe's future is not in the main an American task. The next and final chapter develops criteria for choice in those political-military issues in which there are profitable opportunities for American initiative.

Among the eight ideal-type European security arrangements described in Chapter Four the most clearly inimical to American interests is the Big Finland Western Europe model, in which the states of Western Europe are highly susceptible to Soviet influence.[1] (Its mirror image, the Liberated Eastern Europe model,

---

[1] There are imaginable Western Europes even less desirable than Big Finland Western Europe, e.g., Satellitized Western Europe and Sovietized West-

would be equally inimical to what Soviet leaders perceive as their interests.) Of the other six, three—Two Spheres Europe, Sheltered Western Europe, and Buffer Europe—presuppose that the American nuclear guarantee holds good, and three—WEU Western Europe, Big Sweden Western Europe, and Reconstituted Europe [2]—presuppose that Western Europe no longer needs the guarantee.

The probability is low that by 1980 Western Europe will have acquired the military capability safely to dispense with the American guarantee, but Americans need have no fear of a Western Europe that no longer needs or wants to be under the American nuclear umbrella. A militarily self-sufficient Western Europe could make its own response to the prospect of Soviet conventional or nuclear aggression. And strategic arms limitation would presumably be easier to achieve, because the firebreak between limited (European) war and general war would be territorial rather than technological.[3]

There are many different kinds of European security arrangements with which the United States could live reasonably comfortably. As will be seen, the least comfortable are also the least likely in these last decades of the twentieth century. The range, imperatives, and opportunities for American choice may be examined as they relate to forces for change which neither compel nor permit a

---

ern Europe; but these were judged so unlikely for the 1970s that they were not included among the models described.

[2] If Reconstituted Europe implies a return to a Europe with periodic fratricidal wars, this would not be a Europe the United States could live with, if only because the United States would probably have no better luck in staying out of Europe's future wars than it has had in staying out of its past wars.

[3] Query: Would a European tactical deterrent made possible with American help provide the "territorial firebreak" to replace the technological firebreaks, thus permitting Western Europe's tactical nuclear weapons to balance Soviet conventional superiority? In the next chapter it is argued that deterrence in Europe should rest on conventional forces; but if this is not possible, the question of a Western European nuclear deterrent will be much discussed. As Andrew Pierre's essay, "Britain and European Security: Issues and Choices for the 1970s," in the companion volume, *European Security and the Atlantic System* (New York: Columbia University Press, 1973), points out, the United States–United Kingdom accord on the sharing of nuclear information will have to be renegotiated in the mid-1970s. Any choice the United States might then make to allow France to share nuclear information might be decisive as to the prospect for a European nuclear deterrent.

sharp break with the two-spheres pattern that has survived into the 1970s.

II

"Americans," it is often said, "are the only good Europeans." [4] This wry comment suggests that Americans cannot have any kind of Europe their leaders want and that the range of American choice about Western Europe's future is not unlimited. By sketching what are expected to be enduring features and persisting trends in the European order in the decade ahead and by describing contingencies that it is not within the province of the United States government to control, the range of American choice can be delimited in significant ways.

It is reasonable to assume that the Soviet and American governments continue to perceive the contingency of World War III as truly foreclosed by a system of reciprocal deterrents. Superpower competition will continue, however, in every quarter of the globe. Even so, Europe will remain the theater of most fundamental concern to each superpower. For control by either superpower of its half of Europe to pass to the other superpower would be a cataclysmic event in world politics. For this reason alone, two of the eight model Europes, Big Finland Western Europe and Liberated Eastern Europe—models that describe opposite extremes—are models toward which Europe is very unlikely to move in the 1970s. By contrast, a third unlikely prospect for the near future, a Europe that might emerge after a far-reaching Soviet-American détente—a

---

[4] Atlanticism or "transatlantic federalism" may even seem to the enthusiastic Europeanist to be an obstacle to the development of the European movement and therefore to the emergence of a self-determining, militarily self-sufficient Europe. Some contemporary neo-isolationists argue that the United States ought to disengage from Europe *both* to let (Western?) Europe choose to federate and to concentrate on its own unsolved domestic problems. Whether the states of Western Europe would respond to this shock treatment—dismantling NATO, bringing back American forces from Europe, folding up the nuclear umbrella—by federating and organizing adequately for their defense is doubtful. See, however, David Calleo, *The Atlantic Fantasy* (Baltimore: Johns Hopkins Press, 1970), for the argument of one American who is a "good European."

condominium or Buffer Europe or a Reconstituted Europe from which the superpowers had somehow persuaded each other to "go home"—would continue to exhibit one key characteristic of the Europe of 1970: the self-imposed requirement of each superpower that it not abandon the whole of the Europe that lies between them to the tender mercies of the other.

Neither superpower will withdraw from Europe unless both do or unless sufficient local strength has been built to cope with the other superpower. This last condition is one that Western Europe but not Eastern Europe might conceivably meet. Relations within the two alliance systems are very different, partly (but only partly) because the Soviet Union has no European partners that in another day would have been Great Powers. Whatever the size of the technological gap between the United States and the second-tier powers of the non-Communist world, the West will continue to have an array of such second-tier powers, while the Communist world will have only China in Asia and none in Europe. The regional Great Powers of Western Europe—Britain, France, and West Germany—have no counterpart in Eastern Europe.

For the purposes of this discussion, what is important about this asymmetry is that it may point toward another. It is conceivable that Western Europe will grow strong enough that even if the United States were to discontinue the nuclear commitment to its NATO allies and withdraw its troops from Western Europe, that area would not pass into the other sphere. Eastern Europe, on the other hand, has little chance of developing military power comparable to that of Western Europe, and the Soviet Union cannot cease protecting its Warsaw Treaty allies in Eastern Europe without a grave risk that Eastern Europe would drift into the Western sphere.

In contrast, both WEU Western Europe and Big Sweden Western Europe would meet the minimum United States requirement: no Soviet domination of the Europe presently defended by the American guarantee. How likely Western Europe is to be strong enough to prevent Soviet domination mainly by its own efforts depends on several factors: how much the transatlantic technological gap can be narrowed; how much the high-technology arms race can be slowed down; to what extent West Germany's NATO partners in Europe view its revived power as portending a renewed German threat; how preoccupied the Soviet Union is with a menacing China at its rear; and above all, how willing the peoples of at least the major states of Western Europe are to organize tightly and sacrifice mightily to assure peace and security for themselves without an American guarantee and an American military presence.

The preclusive requirement, that Western Europe not pass to the other side, thus seems certain to remain through the 1970s, whatever formal guarantees and overseas deployments the United States may choose to provide (or withhold). The United States will continue to have at least this minimum commitment to itself. For Americans to mislead themselves—to say nothing of Europe and the Soviet competitor—on this essential point might lead to an otherwise avoidable (and possibly nuclear) war, because the political basis for deterrence would have been destroyed.[5]

The military implications (and the implications for arms control) of this last statement must not be ignored. There should be no ambiguity about what Western European allies are freed from doing by an American defense effort that happens also to protect Western Europe and about what the United States is freed from doing to protect itself because it can safely rely on what its European allies must do in their own interest to defend themselves. For maximum credibility in a Two Spheres Europe, guarantees and deterrents must be based on a preparedness pattern that signals both interdependence of guarantor and guaranteed and the requisite capabilities of each to keep the promises.

The Atlantic Community must therefore remain the organizing concept for American and Western security until the Europe that lies between the superpowers becomes again an autonomous, self-maintaining subsystem in world politics, or until Western Europe by itself becomes such a system. This is a maximum requirement

[5] On the other hand, to be absolutely unambiguous as to the limits of the area beyond which the United States professes no security interest or commitment might be to invite Soviet aggressive action in the adjacent excluded territories.

for the United States, because to ask more is to ask for what the Soviet Union will not passively accept. Visions of a rolled-back Iron Curtain and an Eastern Europe triumphantly liberated belong to the 1950s. It is a minimum condition, because it meets the preclusive test: no Soviet control of Western Europe, whether by conquest or by intimidation.

By this standard, what is meant by a set of *European* security arrangements consonant with American interests? "European security arrangements" means security arrangements for Europe, or at least Western Europe; it does not mean security arrangements from which non-Europeans are excluded. In the period when the cold warriors of each superpower had visions of driving the other superpower entirely out of the Europe that lay between them, the sloganeering of "liberation" and "roll-back" in the West had its counterpart in the East. Thus the preamble of the Warsaw Treaty of 1955 called for "the establishment of a system of collective security in Europe, based on the participation in it of *all European* states" (italics added). Furthermore, Article XI provided for the Warsaw Treaty "to lose its force from the day on which an all-European treaty [on collective security] comes into force." In other words, "all-European" in 1955 meant "Soviet Union in, United States out." By contrast, proposals for a European security conference in the 1970s do not call for negotiations from which the United States would be excluded, with the full consent of Western Europeans. To the extent that the proposed conference deals with security at all, security for political Europe, the Europe that lies between the superpowers, not security for a Soviet-dominated "Europe from the Urals to the Atlantic," must be the theme of any such conference.[6] In the latter Europe the Western half would be cast in the unacceptable Big Finland role.

---

[6] Early Soviet statements in 1970 about the agenda of a European security conference did not suggest that the Soviet Union wished security to be discussed at all. Rather, the emphasis was on legitimizing the de facto settlement that followed World War II. To this, the Western Big Three properly responded by calling for more explicit recognition of the status of West Berlin. In 1972 the Soviet government was prepared to agree to discussion of arms reduction in a subcommittee of the conference.

In the context of this analysis, a fixed requirement of European security is that Western Europe shall not have passed under Soviet domination. Only on this condition can a wider set of European security arrangements provide for a "Europe that lies between the superpowers and is dominated in its entirety by neither."

III

In analyzing the many different kinds of Europe that would not threaten the United States' security and would not require the Soviet Union to accept American hegemony in Eastern Europe, a Two Spheres Europe very much like the Europe of the early 1970s must be the starting point. If the forces that brought the present European security system into being were.certain to persist unchanged for the next decade, Two Spheres Europe might indeed be the only kind of Europe to merit attention.[7] In the near future the Soviet Union seems unlikely to loosen its grip on the Warsaw Treaty countries, and the scope for American initiative in loosening that grip is narrow. As for the West, the vitality of NATO is assured. The United States maintains its entry into Europe; Western Europe gains protection from steps taken to protect American security; and many European governments trust the United States more than some of the other European states.[8] The Western sphere of the two-spheres European security system has at least three other self-maintaining features, which will be considered in turn: the impulse for federation in Western Europe is not strong enough to create a second Western superpower; however successful or unsuccessful the Brandt government's *Ostpolitik* may ultimately be judged, during the next few years Germany will not be reunified,

---

[7] Political forces and trends in military technology may be working in opposite directions so far as Western Europe's future security is concerned, but the effect of the latter changes is over the horizon.

[8] To state the complementary interests of the Atlantic alliance in this way is to suggest why Canadian enthusiasm for NATO has declined. So long as the United States maintains its entry into Europe and Western Europe remains protected, there is little Canadian interest in a specifically Canadian role in determining the pattern of European security.

and resurgent Germany will remain a specter for non-German politicians to conjure with; the expectation of war among the states of Western Europe and North America remains nil.

To restate the argument of earlier chapters, Western Europe has and will continue to have the economic basis to provide for its own military defense against the Soviet Union. The political basis, on the other hand, does not now exist and does not seem to be in prospect. Pressures for nondefense expenditures will rise, and sentiment for Western European federation will remain weak. The economic and technological basis for Western European self-defense is and will be adequate only if the major powers of Western Europe develop common policies to an extent not now foreseeable.[9] Economic trends therefore will continue to permit, but not to compel, a self-sufficient Western European security system. The sentiment for Western European federation or any form of organization for effectively pooling Western Europe's strength is unlikely in the 1970s to be strong enough to harness the area's security potential sufficiently to make NATO and the American guarantee obsolete.

Western European leaders who continue to believe that the Soviet threat to Western security is overriding assume that the Soviet Union is quiescent vis-à-vis Western Europe only because the superior arms and the coalition diplomacy of the NATO countries bar the way and because trouble with China keeps the Soviet Union tied down in Asia. What, however, about Western Europeans who respond to the Soviet call for an "all-European" security system? Some of these may claim to see that Germany is revanchist and that an economically powerful Germany is therefore a dire threat. Portrayal of Germany as the source of the direst threat that "Europe" may be called upon to meet may plausibly be reinforced by any of several other not wholly compatible assumptions: that since the American deterrent against Soviet aggression will protect equally those who do and those who do not pay what the Americans regard as a fair share of Western defense costs, Germany's Western European neighbors can focus *their* attention on the German threat; that whatever formerly may have been the case, the

[9] As explained in Chapter Three, for Western Europe to provide for its own nuclear deterrence full federation is necessary.

Soviet Union is not *now* a threat to Western Europe's security; that the protracted war in Vietnam has raised fundamental doubts about reliance on the United States for ultimate protection against Germany or the Soviet Union; and that the apparent intimacy of German and American policy-makers makes the United States a doubtful ally against an ever more powerful West Germany. These same four assumptions with equal plausibility would reinforce demands for a Sheltered Western Europe (and some of them, in varying combinations, for a Big Sweden Western Europe, for a WEU Western Europe, and for a Reconstituted Europe).

The present military organization of NATO and the earlier abortive efforts to create a European defense community and a multilateral force testify to the political necessity for so organizing the West as to appear to check *both* a real Soviet threat acknowledged by leaders in every NATO country and a potential German threat proclaimed, however unjustly, in some quarters. This will be a continuing need and a continuing problem for the 1970s. This dual requirement has been a problem for the United States although American policy-makers have not themselves for many years viewed Germany as a threat, for the United States' national security policy has sometimes required an alliance with countries in which leading politicians play on mass fears of a revived German threat.[10]

The dual requirement helps to explain why, from the time in 1950 when the United States government first unambiguously advocated German rearmament in high-level negotiations with its major allies, it has continuously supported full American participation in a regional security organization: it has done this in part to assuage European fears of that rearmament. No more than any other government does that of the United States regard alliances and regional security organizations as good in themselves. The presumed Soviet threat seems certain to compel the continued involvement of the United States in Europe, but the organizational

[10] The military organization of the Warsaw Treaty countries also reflects an effort to cope with a dual requirement: to support Soviet policy against the NATO powers and to provide the basis for keeping Soviet forces in Eastern Europe, as instruments for the political control of that area.

form of that involvement depends in the 1970s, as it did in the 1950s and the 1960s, largely on the image of Germany in Europe.

Although all signs point to a continued division of Germany in the 1970s, discrepant views of a future German threat are in fact likely to persist among the NATO allies. No substitute for NATO, however, that does not lock West Germany into a regional security system will be widely acceptable in Western Europe. So long as Europe and Germany in particular remain divided and Western Europe is not strong enough by itself to secure itself against the Soviet Union, the United States has every reason to keep firm its transatlantic security commitment under Article 5 of the North Atlantic Treaty. American armed forces in Germany will then continue not only to serve as hostage forces to give credibility to the American nuclear commitment but also, whether or not so intended, to assure those Western Europeans who fear a revanchist Germany that West German armed forces will not play the dominant role in assuring European security.

So long as these American forces remain, sentiment in the West in favor of turning East for protection against Germany seems unlikely to grow. All this suggests that Western Europe's continued reliance on the American nuclear guarantee is not the only reason why "NATO Western Europe" within the framework of a Two Spheres Europe is likely to persist. A second reason is that the reputed German threat makes NATO Western Europe seem to many Europeans more attractive than an autonomously strong Western Europe. Only in the unlikely event of German reunification could a Reconstituted Europe with its security arrangements directed primarily against a potentially dangerous Germany emerge.

Another feature of the post–World War II world that continues in the 1970s is the minimal prospect of war among the major states of Western Europe. Western Europe is an area within which the major states devote no resources or planning efforts to the possibility of war with each other. This security community is in fact transatlantic, for it includes the United States and Canada.[11] Not

---

[11] Canadian membership in NATO has made NATO look much less like a United States instrument for asserting hegemony over Western Europe and much more like a collective North Atlantic effort.

even the often asserted fear of a revived and revanchist German militarism has led the other great states of Western Europe to plan for the contingency of war with Germany. It will not do so in the 1970s, especially if substantial American forces remain in Germany.

The sentiments that reduce to the vanishing point the specter of war within the North American–Western European region are very different from the attitudes that for centuries before 1945 fueled periodic wars among the Great Powers of Western Europe. These sentiments have not by themselves been sufficient to create "all-in" Western European or North Atlantic political, economic, and military institutions. Nor have they been even sufficient to create functional organizations that include all of the states of Western Europe, as the nonparticipation of Sweden, Switzerland, Spain, and Ireland in NATO and of the first three of these four in the expanded nine-nation Common Market demonstrates. Furthermore, the prospect is nil for an all-in multifunctional organization, whether it be a United States of the North Atlantic or a United States of Western Europe.

States within this security community, however, have and will have a potential for collaboration in functional organizations of varying membership unconstrained by national security calculations vis-à-vis fellow members. The potential remains great for this zone or any part of it to organize to whatever extent shared or complementary interests may be articulated. It is no accident that the functional demand for security was met by creating a transatlantic organization of fifteen countries, while the functional demand for wider trading areas in Europe was met by forming wholly European organizations: the European Common Market, the European Coal and Steel Community, Euratom, and the European Free Trade Association. There is no reason to suppose either that NATO will assume economic functions or that the European economic organizations will assume political-military functions. Sentiments for Atlanticism and for Europeanism may someday be in conflict, but until political, military, and economic functions are to be combined in a single supranational organization, the practical effect of this conflict on Two Spheres Europe will be slight.

The Soviet occupation of Czechoslovakia in 1968 illuminated in a flash many of the continuing realities of the European security problem. It demonstrated once more that the countries in the western alliance are unable or unwilling to moderate the use of force in Soviet–Eastern Europe relations. The Soviet Union took care to make clear what was never really in doubt: that it was posing no new and immediate military threat to the West. Even so, the events of August 1968, by reminding the faint-hearted in the West that Soviet force may well be used against those powerless to oppose it, reactivated old fears of the Soviet Union. Beyond this, the Soviet military intervention in Czechoslovakia seriously weakened the confidence of many people in the belief that critical decisions in Soviet foreign and military policy can be predicted far enough in advance to permit the Western alliance the luxury of not preparing militarily for the worst imaginable contingency. Finally, the intervention underscored a dilemma that each superpower faces as it seeks in Europe to achieve its foreign-policy objectives by a combination of military and nonmilitary means: military means get in the way of nonmilitary means and vice versa.

Soviet military action in Czechoslovakia was an instant local success, but the costs for the Soviet Union in tarnished image were not trivial, especially among Communists and their potential supporters in Western Europe. There are, moreover, less spectacular ways in which the by-product cost of that military action tended to cancel out the apparent security profit. The higher the wall built by military defense the more difficult will be bridge-building to the West with a view to intruding into domestic politics on the other side of the gap. For the Soviet Union and also the United States, steps that seek to achieve security via military action and via dividing the major opponent from its allies or moderating the hostility of its domestic opinion base frequently weaken each other's effectiveness.[12] This is not to say that either superpower can or

---

[12] United States military intervention in the Dominican Republic in 1965 seriously complicated the task of building a nonimperialist image of a benign and pacific United States in the minds of Russians and Eastern Europeans. The United States decisions to halt the flow of military assistance to Greece after a military junta took control and then to restore that flow of military goods demonstrate that the United States has had to pay a price whichever course it has chosen.

should decide to pursue security by only one of the two routes. The effect, however, is to buttress the structure of Two Spheres Europe.

Questioning the credibility of the American nuclear guarantee, which did not stop with the passing of General de Gaulle from the scene, and continuing failure to discover a formula for sharing the defense burden accepted as equitable in both Western Europe and North America seem likely to undermine the foundations of the Atlantic alliance, particularly if the Soviet Union fails to administer one of its periodic shock treatments to the alliance—such as those in Hungary in 1956, in Berlin in 1961, and in Czechoslovakia in 1968. On the other hand, that America's European allies take the trouble to question that credibility is testimony to the value the alliance and the American guarantee have in their eyes and will have, at least until they acquire the military strength to dispense with it. The only circumstance, however, that could evoke much greater Western European sacrifice for rearmament would be a sharply increased fear of Soviet aggression, and this circumstance would also create a sharply increased sense of dependence on the American nuclear guarantee and on NATO. Thus what appear to be the two main threats to Western security organization taking the form of Two Spheres Europe, the problems of credibility and "fair shares," turn out to be self-correcting when and if Soviet-Western relations deteriorate.[13] Suppose, however, arms control is regarded as a variable that may help modify the organization of Western security. Real success in strategic and tactical nuclear arms limitation would make Europe's security turn much more on the balance and organization of conventional arms, with consequences that will later be considered in detail.

What are the possibilities that either side will succeed in promoting splits in the opposing alliance? The limits of Western will (or capacity) to intervene in the Soviet Union's special relationship with its Warsaw Treaty partners have been defined by the military occupation of Czechoslovakia in 1968 and the enunciation of the self-justifying Brezhnev Doctrine. Undoubtedly there is more to at-

[13] This statement assumes that political and military intelligence will remain adequate to provide the warning time necessary for corrective measures.

tract Eastern Europeans in Western Europe than Western Europeans in Eastern Europe, and the magnetism of the West will grow
stronger. With acquiescence on all sides, however, to Soviet military intervention on the basis of the Brezhnev Doctrine, the
technological, cultural, and economic appeal of the West to Eastern Europeans cannot be decisive in modifying the present system
of a two-spheres Europe. On the other hand, even prior to August
1968, the Soviet Union was unpopular in Western Europe among
Right, Center, Social Democratic, and New Left elements and also
even among some of the old Left. No ground swells of opinion in
the West that will compel the present two-spheres Europe to be
modified in ways more agreeable to the Soviet Union than to the
West can be foreseen, nor is there a prospect of any relaxation of
Soviet control over Eastern Europe that would permit a shift in the
opposite direction. More generally, the basic irreconcilability of efforts by the two superpowers to achieve détente among themselves
with efforts by Europeans to achieve détente within Europe
through blurring the present line of division will persist during the
1970s and thus block avenues of rapid movement away from the
Two Spheres pattern.[14]

In summary, no forces in sight will sharply tilt the balance of
East and West or create a great buffer zone between them. Within
the Atlantic alliance economic trends permit but do not require a
somewhat more autonomous organization of Western European security, while the political forces making for continued transatlantic
security arrangements seem stronger than those making for a separate Western European regional security system. On the other
hand, both the distribution of influence within the alliance and the
pattern of sharing the Western defense burden may change substantially in the 1970s.[15]

[14] See Marshall D. Shulman's essay, "The Development of West European
Perceptions of Soviet Policy and Their Implications for European Security," in
Institute of War and Peace Studies, *Arms Control and European Security in
the 1970s: Background Papers* (ACDA/IR-152); Report prepared for the U.S.
Arms Control and Disarmament Agency, November 1971. However, so long
as United States and Soviet efforts to achieve détente are unsynchronized and
alternating, this irreconcilability is unlikely to drive the European allies of
each superpower into the arms of the other.

[15] Zbigniew Brzezinski, in "America and Europe," *Foreign Affairs*, October

IV

In the Europe of the last quarter of the twentieth century America's NATO allies may well have a larger range of choice than they have had in the third quarter. While American dissatisfaction with European foot-dragging may be acute, it seems unlikely to weaken the American nuclear commitment. Basic American strategy is to deter intercontinental nuclear exchange and to keep all other conflict "over there." Thus it is an American perception of the American national interest that keeps American conventional forces and American tactical nuclear power in Europe and that keeps American strategic air and missile power the ultimate guarantor of Western Europe's security. So long as these conditions persist, a decision taken in a moment of irritation to punish ungrateful allies for their slack contribution to the joint defense-deterrent effort would be largely self-defeating.

Furthermore, in the era of reciprocal deterrence and perhaps even more if it is also an era of strategic arms limitation, strong inhibitions on both sides against engaging in thermonuclear war weaken each superpower's ability to restrain its major allies. Thus with the nuclear guarantee remaining firm and credible, the paradox of declining contributions of allies to Western European defense and rising influence of allies in the decisions of the alliance may come to pass. The European allies of the United States have not in any case been allies whose wishes could be ignored. Even

---

1970, asserted that Europeans resent the low estate to which their continent has fallen in the era of Big Two controversy and in what some Europeans think may be worse, the era of Big Two détente. There is a certain inconsistency between the widespread judgment in Europe that there would be no significant European arms buildup to compensate for a unilateral American arms cutback and the expressed resentment that the superpowers may in confrontation *or* collaboration be determining Europe's fate in Europe's absence. Also, there is irony in America's willingness to consult its NATO partners more fully, more routinely, and more systematically being manifested when the prospect of a substantially enlarged Western European defense contribution had come to seem remote. (It is only fair to note that the European Defense Improvement Program of 1970 and the "Europackage" of 1971 have modestly increased the defense contributions of Europe's NATO members as successive arms reductions in the United States have reduced the American share.)

two decades ago, when the United States had a near monopoly of the funds, the goods, and the arms and a mammoth share of the trained military manpower, the European allies could not be commanded. The United States and its NATO allies have gradually learned how to consult with each other, and in the 1970s the United States will have increasing cause to base alliance action on genuine alliance-wide consensus patiently built through full consultation.

Is the United States as free as France or Canada (or any other Atlantic ally) to cut back its troop force levels in Europe without jeopardizing the protection derived from the alliance relationship? The answer seems to be that it is not. For the alliance to remain credible, the leading ally must continue to make good the most serious shortcomings of its partners. Furthermore, to keep the nuclear guarantee credible, American forces must apparently remain in substantial numbers in Europe; they perform a hostage function as well as a defense function. There is rising anti-militarism and neo-isolationism on both sides of the Atlantic and on both sides of the forty-ninth parallel, but its superpower position denies the United States the freedom to respond as completely as its NATO partners to domestic pressures from those who would cut back and decommit.

The prospect then is that the choices of the European NATO allies—Canada has already made its choice—to cut back, maintain, or build up during the 1970s will determine the amount of movement away from a Two Spheres Europe toward one in which leadership by the United States is less marked, consultation by the United States is more marked, and the European contribution is somewhat reduced—i.e., toward a Sheltered Western Europe variant.

In burden-sharing the partner who cares less has an advantage, and the partner for whom "the buck stops here" has a disadvantage. But the European powers who choose to care more could undoubtedly have a very different kind of advantage, given the rising anti-militarist sentiment in the United States and the problems of inflation and balance of payments. A larger contribution to the common NATO defense by any of them would purchase much influence over American policy, and every successive increment still more influence.

What choices these second-tier powers of Western Europe make and how they choose depend on what threats each perceives to its own and Western Europe's security. In the 1970s these perceptions will be significantly influenced by the transformations in the strategic balance discussed in Chapter Two and in particular by Western European (and American) perceptions of the import of strategic parity for the reliability of the American nuclear commitment. The argument is made in the next chapter that the nature of the Soviet threat and its relationship to American strategic superiority and to the American military presence in Europe have been largely misperceived or at any rate not fully reflected by existing arms policies and military doctrine. These misperceptions, if uncorrected, may hasten the drift from a Two Spheres Europe toward a Sheltered Western Europe variant, a variant that Americans would find more costly and less efficient. More to the point for present purposes, these misperceptions, by assigning too much importance to changes in the strategic balance, may divert attention from the critical arms control problems associated with European security.

V

This then is Europe's future in the years ahead: a United States that cannot allow the whole of Europe to pass under Soviet hegemony; a two-spheres set of European security arrangements with many self-maintaining features; a possible drift toward a Sheltered or free-ride Western Europe that the United States cannot halt except by bringing its European alliance partners to perceive the costs to themselves of such a drift.

A few general remarks about that future are in order before the next chapter considers actual choices open to American policymakers. These points are necessary to clarify how American choices relate to future security arrangements for Europe and especially for Western Europe.

The first point is to reiterate that the opportunity for American choices to shape this European future is at best limited. In the fu-

ture as in the past, the development of European security arrangements will be influenced by the actions and conceptions of Soviet
and European leaders as well as by those of the American government. The point seems to be banal, except for the fact that in the
past the American government on more than one occasion has
acted on the premise that its wishes could be horses if only all the
members would saddle up the same horse and ride it in the same
direction. This, in itself, is an unlikely contingency, but it is worth
remembering that even on those rare occasions when Washington
has reached a consensus on the direction in which it wished to see
Western Europe develop, it has rarely met with total success.

A second important and equally obvious point is that the future
will be reached incrementally rather than by one great step or
sweeping policy conception. SALT, the tortuous exchanges to determine the format and agenda of the Soviet-proposed European
security conference, the recurring debate about the role and level
of American forces in Europe and its relation to mutual balanced
force reduction, the labors of the NATO Nuclear Planning Group
on tactical nuclear weapons doctrine, Anglo-American talks in the
mid-1970s on the renewal of nuclear aid arrangements—these are
only some of the strands out of which the fabric of future European security will be woven gradually. Although each of these individual opportunities for choice (and the many more that will
exist) may be perceived at the time by the American officials concerned as *the* critical turning point, not one of them will really be
such.

Nonetheless, through a succession of choices by the American
government and the governments of European nations and the Soviet Union, by the end of the decade a future will have been
reached. The opportunities of the American government to shape
this future will be limited, but they will not be without some effect. Accordingly, if this effect is not to be dissipated, the American
government will need some conception of the best of all feasible
security arrangements toward which it would hope to see Europe
move.

The United States government, as has been demonstrated, can
afford to be rather flexible in its conception of desirable, feasible

futures. The American military stake in the European balance of power is essentially one of denial: although it remains vital for American security that the Soviet Union does not secure command over the people and resources of Western Europe, it is not essential that the United States enjoy such a command. So far as American military security is concerned, none of the possible model Europes discussed in this study, with the exception of Big Finland Western Europe, is totally unacceptable.

The American interest lies not so much in which of these Europes the future brings but in the manner in which the future comes. The prime requirement for American foreign policy is that it not appear to get in the way of futures toward which the Europeans themselves desire to move.

The first chapter of this book discussed the American stake in Europe solely in terms of the problems that would follow from Soviet command over the military capabilities of the continent. The American stake in Europe, both west and east, is actually far broader than that. American security is a function not only of the military capabilities of the Soviet Union but also of the political interests and perspectives that guide the actions of the leaders of the Soviet Union. In a thermonuclear age the best that the United States can hope to do by developing this or that new weapons system or strategy for itself and its NATO allies is to prevent a deterioration in the American security position. There is little prospect that the development of new weapons systems and strategies will significantly improve the American security position.

That improvement, if it comes, will result from changes in the ideas that Soviet leaders entertain about the nature of the international political process and the behavior to be expected of various actors in that process. The last two decades have seen a number of consequential changes in the ideas that Soviet leaders have about international relations: the end of the "fatalistic inevitability" of war between the Soviet Union and capitalist states, an increased emphasis on prospects for nonviolent transformations from capitalism to socialism, and a growing sophistication about the manner in which American foreign policy is made. Changes of this order have facilitated somewhat the opportunity for the two superpowers to live peacefully on the same planet. It is doubtful that at the end of the next decade the then current Soviet leaders will be moved by exactly the same political interests and perspectives as those of the present leadership. There will be some change, although that these changes will make easier the task of peaceful coexistence is certainly not given.

It is in this area that future developments in Europe may make their greatest contribution to American security. The quality of social, economic, and political life within European states and political relations among them constitute a showcase of behavior that may serve in time to confound, refute, and modify some of the central tenets of Marxist-Leninism. To be sure, nothing is harder to move than an idea once implanted in a human mind. But the interests and perspectives that move statesmen do change and with the exception of the quality of life within the United States itself, there is probably no other set of political, economic, and social events toward which the ideas of Soviet leaders are likely to be more responsive than those in Western Europe.

A Western Europe that the Russians can perceive as moving freely toward its own conception of a desirable, feasible future (without an overbearing and contentious American presence)—provided that the future serves to enhance the prosperity, dignity, and freedom of individual Europeans and continues to be characterized by neither fear of war among the Western European states nor fear of Soviet military blackmail—is a Europe that will make a marked contribution to American security, however that Europe is formally structured.

/ Chapter Seven

pERspectives and choices
foR aRms contRol

I

THE PURPOSE OF THIS CHAPTER is to outline some decisions that the United States might make on the military and arms
control issues that will be associated with the future development
of European security arrangements. In particular, the chapter is
addressed to the question of what the United States can do, given
its nuclear commitment to Western Europe, to reduce the strain
that this commitment imposes on the Soviet-American balance of
terror without at the same time increasing the strain on security arrangements for Western Europe.

The chapter thus returns to the strategic dilemma described at
the start of this book, with the object of searching for perspectives
and choices that may ease that dilemma in the 1970s. As the intervening chapters have shown, the issue cannot be avoided. The
1970s will see neither a Western Europe able to provide for its
own defense nor a United States unwilling to defend the area by
the threat of nuclear war. On the other hand, unless the United
States is prepared to renew the strategic arms race, the new Soviet-American nuclear balance (especially if it is codified with a

SALT agreement) may undermine the confidence of the Western Europeans in both the will and the ability of the United States to deliver on that threat.

The policy problem that therefore confronts the United States is how to provide the kind of military forces and strategy to meet its nuclear guarantee that will seem at the same time credible to the Western Europeans and nonprovocative to the Russians. The answers advanced in this chapter take as their points of departure an analysis of the relationship between the character of the strategic balance and the effectiveness of the nuclear guarantee to Western Europe and the argument that the deterrent effect of that guarantee is less dependent on American superiority than many Americans and Western Europeans have heretofore presumed. Subsequent sections of the chapter describe some choices that could be made in the light of this analysis among arms and arms control policies for America's strategic forces and for NATO's tactical nuclear and conventional forces. The chapter closes with some summary perspectives on future European security arrangements and American interests.

II

Few would contest the proposition that in the 1970s, as in the decade before, there will be nothing that the Soviet Union could hope to gain from an attack on Western Europe that would be worth the costs of a nuclear war. The difficulty with this proposition as far as the effectiveness of American nuclear deterrence is concerned lies not with its validity but with its relevance.

There has been a rather poor intellectual fit between deterrence theory and the actual conditions under which statesmen decide on war. Deterrence theory rests on the assumption that these choices are made after a determination of the costs that war would bring and that statesmen, after carefully weighing these expected costs against the value of the objects that could be gained by war, decide on war or peace depending on whether the expected costs seem to offset or not the expected gains. There is little evidence to indicate that statesmen have ever made war or peace choices in this manner, and it is difficult to see how they could if they wanted to. Statesmen are not capable of making such judgments, for there is no calculus by which they can weigh their political objects in terms of human lives or even industrial capacity.[1]

In reality most statesmen, at least in the twentieth century, have moved toward war as a result of policies for which they had decided only to *risk* the costs of war, and they have decided on war itself only as a result of the belief that their political choices had narrowed down to war now or war later. In neither event is the absolute level of fatalities statesmen may expect the war to bring particularly relevant to their calculations. If the choice is only to risk the costs of war, statesmen can avoid a judgment about whether their objects are worth actually incurring those costs. And if the choice is perceived to be between war now or war later, decisions will be reached through reference to relative, not absolute, costs.[2]

These conditions provide cause for both concern and confidence so far as the continued effectiveness of the American nuclear commitment to Western Europe is concerned. The grounds for concern result from the fact that while neither superpower has objects that will lead it to want to incur the costs of nuclear war, both have objects for which they may be willing to risk those costs. Indeed, neither the Soviet Union nor the United States appears to have been as inhibited about risking the costs of nuclear war as were the British and French in the 1930s about risking again the costs of World

[1] How, for example, could one decide how many lives the War of 1812 or the War against Mexico was worth? The issue needs research, but it is doubtful that statesmen in earlier centuries ever thought of war in these terms.

[2] American policy on the eve of World War II provides some relevant, if not encouraging, precedents for the nuclear age. Franklin Roosevelt was a humane and conscientious leader, but he could do better than be guided by the crude speculation that the costs of war now would be less than the costs of war later (thus his determination to help Britain defeat Hitler was grounded in the expectation that a victorious Germany would next turn to the Western Hemisphere) or base his policy on the hope that the costs of war could be avoided altogether by a firm threat to fight it (thus while Roosevelt was willing to risk war with Japan, his object was to deter her). Note, however, that since Roosevelt's choice was only to risk the costs of war with Japan, neither he nor his advisers ever confronted the question of just how much American blood and treasure the defense of China and Southeast Asia was worth.

War I. A succession of Berlin crises, the Cuban missile crisis, and the American NATO commitment itself would seem to support this point. The danger of course lies in the possibility that in the clash of policies that risk the cost of nuclear war, one or both powers may come to believe that its choices have narrowed down to war now or war later, for in this event, as noted, the unprecedented level of the absolute costs involved will cease to be relevant.

On the other hand, these same conditions also insure that the willingness of the United States to risk nuclear war in defense of Western Europe and the effectiveness of that commitment would prove less sensitive to the disappearance of American strategic superiority than many have believed. To begin with, the advent of parity would not affect the American countercity capability, and thus the costs of nuclear war for the Soviet Union would remain essentially unchanged. The military effect of parity would be to diminish the American counterforce capability and thus its opportunity to reduce the costs of a Soviet strike. But even a very large reduction in American damage-limiting ability (e.g., one which would increase fatalities resulting from a Soviet strike from 30 percent to 60 percent of the American population) would be difficult to relate to future policy. Since decisions to risk the costs of war are made in any event without a direct judgment about whether the policy objects would be actually worth such costs, American willingness to risk the costs of nuclear war in defense of Western Europe will not be significantly affected by changes in the extent of those costs.

The key factor in the continued effectiveness of the American nuclear deterrent is political commitment, not expected damage. So long as the American commitment to Western Europe remains clear and there is a large American military presence in Europe to italicize that commitment, the Soviet Union has every reason to believe that an all-out assault on Western Europe would lead the United States to conclude that it was confronted with the stark choice of nuclear war now or nuclear war later. Since the content of American plans, organizational inertia, and the structure of the strategic problem would all point toward the choice of war now, the prospect of such an assault seems fantastically remote, especially when viewed against the circumspect conduct of Soviet policy over the past two decades.

Indeed there are no apparent political reasons why the Soviets could be expected to launch an all-out assault on Western Europe even if they should assign a very low or zero probability to the prospect of an American strategic nuclear response. Nations have been deterred before by less devastating prospects than nuclear demolition, and the conventional and tactical nuclear forces presently available to NATO would seem to provide Western Europe with a very formidable raincoat, even if the American strategic umbrella should fold in the storm. "Victory" would promise the Soviet Union little more than access to a ruined, resentful, and radioactive Western Europe along lines of communications that ran through a ruined, resentful, and radioactive Eastern Europe. Moreover, the Soviet Union would also have to confront the prospective actions of a United States that had decided *not* to let loose its strategic nuclear weapons. Such an American decision would reflect the conclusion that it would be better to fight a nuclear war later, and the Soviet Union could anticipate the harnessing of the superior American gross national product to an all-out effort to develop an overwhelming capability for offensive and defensive nuclear war. This would present the Soviet Union with the choice of either entering into an unbelievably desperate and expensive arms race or awaiting a future in which destruction from a nuclear exchange would be very asymmetrical. Neither prospect would be appealing to Soviet leaders, and these prospects would surely exercise a deterrent effect on any decision to launch an all-out assault on Western Europe.

The same reasoning points to the lack of political realism behind various scenarios envisioning a Soviet *coup de main* on the flanks of NATO. The Soviets have the military capability to seize such areas, but even if the Soviet Union were assured that it could make such a move without provoking all-out nuclear war, the Politburo would still have to contemplate the character of subsequent American and Western European actions. Given continued American commitment to Western Europe and continued NATO unity, the Politburo would have to anticipate that such a use of force, even if not met directly, would set in motion a series of political and military actions upon the part of the United States and its allies that would lead in the end to a net loss in the Soviet security position. Anticipated reactions of this order constitute "political deterrence." They are as much a part of NATO defenses as on-line divisions or strategic missiles, and any analysis of the security of Western Europe that fails to take account of such political deterrence is incomplete and unrealistic.[3]

It is important to note finally that if the Soviet Union should initiate the use of force in Western Europe, the Soviet action would not reflect a "real" failure of deterrence in the sense that the Soviet Union had decided to incur the costs of nuclear war. Given the continuation of Two Spheres Europe or a Sheltered Western Europe variant, a Soviet use of force could only be the result of a miscalculation regarding the American commitment to some part of the status quo or a mistaken belief that the United States was itself trying to alter the status quo. In either event, the political problem would be to untangle the misunderstanding.

It follows that the United States and its allies need to design both their military forces and their military doctrine to suit this political need. What is required, in the event of violence in Western Europe, is not a war-fighting capability but a war-delaying capability, not a war-winning strategy but a war-ending strategy. For these political purposes, parity in strategic nuclear forces will prove as useful as superiority. What will be required is a strategy for the limited use of nuclear weapons and the command and control systems to execute it, and this is a capability that can be achieved on the basis of strategic equality as well as superiority.

To summarize, the key element in the security of Western Europe is the American political commitment to defend it, and the

---

[3] One may ask what deters Soviet military action in non-NATO, non-Communist Europe, i.e., in areas west of the dividing line that are not now formally protected by Article 5 of the North Atlantic Treaty and the American nuclear guarantee—for example, Finland and Sweden. Here "political deterrence" is operating; short-term Soviet military gains would trigger a gigantic rearmament throughout the NATO area and impose on the Soviet Union a critical choice: to acquiesce, to rearm competitively, or to escalate conflict in the Nordic countries into World War III.

deterrent effect of this commitment would not be significantly altered by the advent of strategic parity, whether by result of the arms race or by an arms control agreement. But this is a contingent analysis. The continued effectiveness of NATO deterrence is also dependent on the size and quality of the alliance's conventional and tactical nuclear forces. The analysis here has assumed that the American political commitment will continue to be symbolized by a large conventional presence in Western Europe and that the alliance's tactical nuclear forces are designed to reflect the need for a war-ending, war-delaying strategy. The first condition may not be met in the future, and the second may not be met even in the present.

In an era, therefore, in which the Soviet-American strategic balance is perceived politically as one of equality, NATO policies for conventional and tactical nuclear forces pose critical problems and choices. The analysis of these issues will be facilitated if consideration is given first to some general perspectives on arms control policy and their application to policies for strategic forces.

III

The fanfare attending the Strategic Arms Limitation Talks suggests to the uninitiated that arms control is a one-time event and that its hour has come. But arms control is a process, not an event, and the process of arms control must continue no matter how great the success or abysmal the failure of SALT or of a future European security conference. Strategic arms limitation, important as it is, is not the only or even the most consequential arms control problem facing the United States in the 1970s. There will continue to be plenty for arms control policy to do, whatever successes the conversations begun in Vienna and Helsinki may from time to time achieve.

It would be a mistake, moreover, to rely solely on formally negotiated arms control agreements to meet these problems. To begin with, formal arms control is not the overriding concern of Soviet policy-makers, as they demonstrated when they destroyed the possibility of strategic arms control negotiations in 1968 by their military intervention in Czechoslovakia. Formal arms control has no absolute priority in the United States either, as was shown by the Nixon Administration's initial interest in tying the opening of SALT to progress on a Middle East settlement and to other issues.

A second difficulty with formal arms control agreements is that some problems are more open to this approach than others, and to date at least, the less formidable problems have proven to be the more amenable. The prospect of a war and a public-health menace nobody wanted helped to produce the hot line and the limited test-ban treaty. But there is no guarantee that a conversation over the hot line will prove any more effective in preventing war than the 1914 "Willy-Nicky" correspondence over the telegraph proved to be, and the holes permitted by the test-ban treaty proved big enough to permit the development of a whole new generation of nuclear warheads. Similarly, the import of agreements to ban nuclear weapons in outer space and Antarctica must be weighed against the inability of the superpowers to find any persuasive military reasons for putting weapons there.

The recently ratified nonproliferation treaty is a further example of an "easy" arms control agreement. The superpowers are finding the going harder at SALT, as they search for agreeable ways to limit their own nuclear weapons,[4] and they might find the going even harder if they moved from a discussion of strategic nuclear weapons to an effort to limit tactical nuclear weapons systems and conventional arms. These are arms control problems that also must be negotiated with allies, for Washington cannot seek the holy grail of arms-controlled détente no matter what the cost in insecurity to its allies.[5]

[4] A formal agreement is especially difficult to reach if (as in a MIRV ban or a limitation of SS-9s) it would trade off the fruits of one side's technological leadership for a commitment from the other side not to plant the seeds for a future leadership.

[5] Arms limitations that are easy to achieve because they are popular at home and advantageous to a potential opponent may not be wise. With both selective service and unbalanced budgets unpopular, negotiating some kinds of *balanced* conventional-force reductions may be difficult. The other side will inevitably trade on popularity in the United States for any kind of conventional-arms limitation for which the negotiators can claim with a shadow of plausibility a balance in reductions. Conversely, where the exchange ratio is very

Progress on formal arms limitaton will therefore at best proceed in fits and starts. Moreover, in a world of dynamic technology the effectiveness of detailed, formal agreements is inherently short-lived. They obsolesce along with the technology being regulated.

It follows that the possibilities for arms self-control, especially when it may lead to tacitly accepted mutual restraints, need to be as energetically explored as the possibilities for formally negotiated arms agreements.[6]

In the past two decades, the United States government has appeared singularly insensitive to the opportunities and need for arms self-control. American technological virtuosity has on occasion been used to postpone or evade difficult political problems. Thus the present heavy reliance on tactical nuclear weapons for the defense of Western Europe, a reliance which poses a host of arms limitation problems, results from a North Atlantic Council decision made in 1954. The New Look and related policies in other NATO countries generated pressure for conventional arms cutbacks inconsistent with fulfilling NATO force goals set at Lisbon in 1952. This pressure was met by a politically convenient decision to use tactical nuclear weapons to make up the conventional-force deficiency.

It is of course prudent to design weapons for the worst possible future envisioned at the time, and subsequent events have demonstrated in some cases the wisdom of taking care not to dissipate essential lead time.[7] But time and again weapons and weapons sys-

---

favorable to the United States and the other side's shoe pinches, the United States can charge a high price for accepting some particular arms limitations, perhaps by asking for some compensatory acceptance of an arms limitation that the United States particularly desires.

[6] This statement has important implications for the way in which the United States government is currently organized to make arms control policy. The matter is outside the terms of reference for this study, but the following questions deserve notice: Is the arms control policy process today such that it can utilize with equal effectiveness whichever of the three paths toward control—formal agreement, tacit agreement, and self-control—seems the most promising in achieving any particular arms limitation? If not, is there a built-in organizational bias toward control by formal agreement?

[7] The classic case of a decision to base national security on exploitation of technological and scientific leadership rather than on arms self-control was the

tems have continued to be perfected, developed, and deployed in the better future that actually materialized. As the United States may yet learn to its sorrow at SALT, the production and deployment of weapons prudently developed for a winter of confrontation can blight a spring of negotiation, and by blighting that future the weapons may have generated insecurity rather than security. Certainly the United States has provided the Soviet Union with provocative precedents. If Americans need weapons to cope with a greater than expected threat (GET), if Americans need the means to produce multiple assured destruction (MAD), and if Americans need a capability of firing first if necessary (COFFIN), what can Russians be expected to learn from the American example?

Not every potential in military technology needs to be translated into a fully deployed weapons system, especially if the system's main foreign-policy effect is to communicate a threatening intention its possessor does not have. A special problem for American arms self-control may be a kind of technological hubris leading to an often false belief that tomorrow's technological breakthrough is more dependable than today's arms control. (We are certain to turn something up; they may cheat.) The United States does not in fact often have to make *this* choice. The critical choice may be at the advanced development–prototype or the production–early deployment stage. Here the argument is that the American taxpayer would never stand for the "waste" of abandoning a proven military capability for a speculative arms limitation. "Staying ahead" may sometimes be the best available option, but more often it may be costly and even dangerous.

Why not try the experiment of encouraging the Soviet government instead to engage in reciprocal arms self-control? And what other way is there to make this experiment except by Americans practicing rigorous arms self-control themselves and seizing every

---

decision of the Truman administration to try to produce a hydrogen bomb. Some of President Truman's advisers were highly sensitive to the arms self-control opportunities thereby foregone. In this case as in many others the "safe" thing appeared to be to proceed with research and development. See Warner R. Schilling, "The H-Bomb Decision: How to Decide without Actually Choosing," *Political Science Quarterly* (March, 1961), pp. 24–46.

opportunity to help the Russians understand what military capabilities the United States has deliberately chosen not to possess and what imagined or imaginable military threats from the United States are thereby demonstrated to be without substance?

Arms self-control and an active arms dialogue are inextricably related. Arms self-control that does not stimulate arms self-control on the other side will be limited in effect and politically infeasible over time. Arms self-control must be real, not disingenuous; and it must be well publicized, well explained, and well understood on the other side. Only then can it strengthen the hands of those in the Soviet government who also may wish to practice rigorous self-control, whether by virtue of their worries about the demands on the Soviet economy from their own "metal eaters," their fears about a contingent Chinese threat, or their own concern for consequences of an uncontrolled strategic arms race.

But before arms self-control can be imitated by the Soviet Union, it must first be started by the United States, and before the United States can initiate a continuous strategic dialogue with Moscow, that dialogue must first be joined in Washington.[8] Americans need to reexamine both the strategic rationale for GET, MAD, and COFFIN and the political consequences these policies may entail. Americans also need to understand better under what circumstances these policies provide additional insurance against Soviet military forces and under what circumstances they provide an added incentive for Soviet forces to multiply. Americans also need to appreciate that the case for any given arms control measure is not refuted merely by showing that its effectiveness may be uncertain or that risks and dangers may attend its implementation. There is also uncertainty, risk, and danger in a future characterized by continued, unchecked weapons development and deployment. Safety lies in the direction of choosing the lesser risks and dangers.

---

[8] This statement can be turned around. The United States cannot respond to a Soviet demonstration of arms self-control until the Soviet Union has desisted from arming itself in some observable way. An alternative path to mutual restraint based on tacit agreement is to take care to note every sign of Soviet arms restraint and respond promptly in kind whenever appropriate.

To exploit fully the opportunities for arms self-control, Americans arms controllers will have to find improved ways to translate into actual policy their theoretical appreciation that there are some weapons without which both sides would be better off. Those responsible for arms control need a capability for monitoring new weapons developments from the very beginning, with regard both to their technical prospects and to their import for the strategic balance, so that the controllers can make an early determination about the desirability and feasibility of subjecting these new weapons to either arms self-control or negotiated arms limitation. In this connection Washington might well profit from some retrospective analysis of the question of why MIRV came so late to the national arms control agenda and how carefully at various stages of MIRV's career the possible benefits of slowing down or halting its development or deployment were examined.

Although some might see Secretary McNamara's tenure in the Department of Defense as the golden years of lost opportunities for arms self-control, the emerging weapons technology of the late 1970s will not be without its own possibilities. In a period when fixed-site ICBMs of both superpowers will become increasingly vulnerable, the contribution that submarine-launched weapons can make toward reducing the strain to preempt in time of crisis seems sufficiently impressive to give both superpowers an interest in exploring ways to forestall the development of more effective anti-submarine warfare technology. Similarly, since it may not be in the interest of either superpower for CEPs to get even smaller, this could provide the incentive for exploring the possibility of improving unilateral inspection technology to the point where each superpower could monitor the other's self-restraint.

To summarize, the Soviet and American governments do not face only the choice between an uncontrolled arms race on the one hand and negotiated arms limitations on the other. There is also a third way: an effort to achieve a more stable military environment in Europe and in the world though better communication and self-control—communication in the form of a continuing strategic dialogue, and self-control in the forms of arms self-restraint (demonstrated by not preparing for unreal nightmares and nonexistent enemy capabilities) and of selective arms acquisition (making available force more finely adjusted to one's own political intentions and to the need to prevent the other side's miscalculations).

IV

The success with which the United States can practice arms self-control will be critical not only for the strategic balance in the 1970s but also for European security arrangements. The need for dialogue regarding arms and the opportunities for self-restraint are not restricted to the confrontation of Soviet and American strategic power; they are equally relevant to the confrontation between NATO and the Warsaw Treaty Organization in Central Europe. Nor can policies for either confrontation afford to be developed without reference to the other. The greater the stability of the European balance the less is the strain on the Soviet-American strategic balance, since the pressure on the United States to backstop Western Europe's defenses with an imbalance of terror in America's favor is accordingly reduced. On the other hand, as noted earlier, pressures in the early 1970s for new expenditures for strategic weapons (even if SALT results in a limited arms control agreement) may intensify pressures for excessive reduction in America's contribution to NATO's conventional forces and thus lead to an imbalance of power on the Continent, unless those pressures are checked by a conscious effort at arms control.

The prospective strain on the stability of present European security arrangements would be slight if there was any assurance that the Western Europeans would match reductions in American conventional forces with increases in their own.[9] The United States has nothing to fear and everything to gain from a Western Europe prepared to assume the burden of its own defense. But however at-

[9] Many (perhaps most) Western European observers of the American scene watch the current debate regarding United States force reductions in Europe as if its outcome were beyond the possibility of any change as a result of European actions. Evoking the kind of conditional support for arms or for arms reduction that increases the Soviet interest in mutual reductions and decreases American support for unilateral arms and troop reductions is a problem of alliance policy.

tractive the vision to the United States of a WEU Western Europe or even a Big Sweden Western Europe, there are no pressures that the United States effectively can apply to move Western Europe toward either of these outcomes.[10] These are futures for the Western Europeans to choose, and there is little reason to expect them to take initiatives leading toward either form of a militarily strong Western Europe. There also is little prospect that the superpowers, especially the Soviet Union, will lessen their roles in their respective halves of Europe in the 1970s by negotiating the kind of détente that would signal the emergence of a Buffer Europe and perhaps in time lead toward an autonomous Reconstituted Europe.

Given the erosion of any widespread belief either in Washington or on the Continent in the possibility of an all-out Soviet assault on Western Europe, the NATO powers will find it difficult to maintain the force levels or to sustain the interest in defense planning that have characterized the past two decades. Even among those who believe that the Soviets once harbored the ambition to make such an assault, few do today, and still fewer may tomorrow. On the other hand, although the expectation of violence has decreased, no corresponding convergence in the character of the political arrangements preferred by Washington and Moscow for Europe has occurred. The prospects for a mutually agreeable settlement of the division of Germany, for example, remain remote. Moreover, the policies of the Soviet Union since the end of World War II demonstrate that it, no less than the United States, has by no means renounced the use of force as an instrument for achieving preferred political arrangements.

Accordingly, the NATO powers will confront the problem of how to reduce military forces without presenting the Soviet Union with opportunities it may be tempted to seize, moved either by ambitions only temporarily thwarted or by memories of a previous era of hostility and fear of its return. This problem can be illustrated by reference to the most "favorable" conception of past So-

[10] Some drastic Soviet action might move the NATO partners on both sides of the Atlantic to rearm, but this kind of strengthened Western Europe would not be disposed to assert Western European independence vis-à-vis the United States.

viet military policy: that the Soviet Union never entertained any real ambition to make a military assault on Western Europe, but rather maintained a large land capability for the purpose of holding Western Europe hostage for America's good behavior. If this in fact had been the rationale for Soviet military policy, Soviet leaders might then have seen the "true" purpose of NATO as preparation for aggression against the Soviet Union. Against such a background of fear and suspicion, should the power and unity of the North Atlantic alliance appreciably deteriorate in the 1970s, the Soviet Union might be disposed to pursue political and military policies that would be indistinguishable on their face from those it might follow if it had all along entertained aggressive ambitions toward Western Europe.

This is not to state that arms reduction and alliance deterioration before a nonaggressive but still fearful Soviet Union would prove as dangerous as disarmament and division before a hostile and expansionist Soviet Union, nor to resurrect the all-out Soviet assault buried earlier in this chapter. The point is that the present political status quo is not an optimum for the Soviet Union, and if the distribution of power on the Continent should significantly change, even a security-conscious Soviet Union might be expected to consider military policies that would exploit that change or probe that status quo.[11]

[11] Paradoxically, a modest reduction in NATO forces might produce an improvement in military effectiveness. A reduction in budgets could provide the incentive for a more economic allocation of military resources among NATO powers, and a reduction in forces the incentive for innovation in doctrine. It is now more than two decades since the end of World War II, yet NATO doctrine (and that of WTO even more) still seems preoccupied with the vision of a land war determined by the movement of armored divisions supported by tactical air forces across the northern European plain. It is at least possible that technological developments since the end of World War II—increased fire power of small units, new forms of mobility, and revolutionary developments in the technology for intelligence and command and control—would lend themselves to doctrinal innovations as radical as those introduced by the Germans in 1940.

The difficulty with new doctrine, as this example illustrates, is that it has no deterrent value. By virtue of its "newness" it is doctrine that may not have occurred to the Soviet Union and therefore will not affect Soviet expectations about the military outcome of battle. Nonetheless, development of greater mil-

A primary task for American arms control policy in the 1970s therefore will be to contribute to the maintenance of a Two Spheres Europe and to prevent or at least minimize movement toward its close but less desirable variant, Sheltered Western Europe. On its part the Soviet Union can be expected to do what it can to facilitate movement toward Sheltered Western Europe because of the potential strain that this arrangement will put on the Western alliance. But otherwise Two Spheres Europe may also appear to the Soviet Union as the best feasible European future for the 1970s. Big Finland Western Europe will presumably be judged as unobtainable as it is attractive, and the major alternatives— WEU Western Europe, Big Sweden Western Europe, and Reconstituted Europe—may look in the Soviet perspective like Big Germany Europe.

There are four objectives for American arms control policy in a Two Spheres Europe: (1) a military posture on both sides that neither threatens nor invites an all-out attack; (2) a political commitment by both sides to the territorial status quo that ideally is clear enough to deter the use of force, but in any event is strong enough to lead both sides to expect that if force should ever be used, it could only reflect some confusion about the identity of the status quo or a mistaken belief that one side had challenged the status quo; (3) a recognition by both sides that in the event of a clash of arms their military need will be to confine and restrict the violence until politicians can identify and unravel the miscalculations that started it; (4) a deliberate effort by both sides to develop military dispositions, doctrine, and weapons that will permit each to engage in acts of restraint without gravely jeopardizing the military security of either its own or the other's forces.

These objectives will not be easily attained, and they certainly cannot be reached through one overall arms control agreement.

---

itary effectiveness would be of considerable utility, for the purpose of NATO's conventional forces (given a war-delaying, war-terminating strategy) will be not to "win" a big land battle in Europe but to insure that local use of force on the part of the Soviet Union will result in the smallest immediate change in the status quo and provide the time for the NATO powers to persuade the Soviet Union that it has misjudged the value they attach to such a change.

They will require continuous and imaginative effort, month by month and year by year. They will also require negotiations in a variety of political arenas. Some arrangements will lend themselves to discussion between the superpowers, either bilaterally or in the more general forum of a European security conference. Other arrangements will be best achieved through negotiations between Washington and its NATO allies, and some of the most important arrangements will require mainly that Washington negotiate with itself.

V

At present, apart from agreement on strategic weapons, most of the arms control arrangements pertaining to Europe that might be feasibly negotiated with the Soviet Union would have mainly atmospheric value: a nonaggression pact between NATO and WTO; a hot line between their major military headquarters; established procedures for exchanging information on troop maneuvers and deployment; arrangements for the periodic exchange of visits between headquarters; establishment of a NATO-WTO arms control group. An agreement on any or all of these items would nonetheless be useful, for they would help to symbolize a commitment to the status quo and an interest in the development of escalation-preventing and war-terminating policies. Moreover, by improving the flow of information between the two sides, these agreements could be steps toward mutually understood and reciprocated arms self-control.

Most of these issues are as appropriate for discussion at a European security conference as in Big Two talks. The pressure for such a conference from the allies of both the United States and the Soviet Union can be expected to mount as progress is made on strategic arms agreements. Moreover, the arms control case for holding such a conference might be even stronger should the SALT negotiations stalemate at any point. The reasons for a failure at SALT would not necessarily be relevant to the issues on the agenda of a European security conference, and it might be useful to moderate the alarm and despair that would attend a stalemate with a conference that would accent the common interest of the superpowers in the continued stability of Two Spheres Europe. At all events, there is certainly no need for the United States to assess the potential of a European security conference in terms of the narrow agenda first proposed by the Soviet Union or to appear a reluctant, foot-dragging participant, for the Western Europeans can be relied upon to resist an agenda that has no other point than to encourage the Americans to withdraw from Europe.

In planning for a European security conference the United States needs to be sensitive to the fact that the interests of the allies in such a conference are not limited to the prospects for formal agreements between the two European security organizations. The politicians in several Western European countries (and some in Eastern Europe as well) may see the forum of a general security conference also as an opportunity for improving their political-bureaucratic positions at home and as a means of influencing the policies of their superpower ally.

This view explains the growing interest in Western Europe for general negotiations on "mutual balanced force reductions." The fear that the United States may soon feel compelled to make "unilateral unbalanced troop reductions" has made formal negotiations on MBFR look very attractive to the exposed NATO allies in Europe (especially the West Germans), if only as a means of making it harder for the Americans to engage in UUFR while negotiations are taking place.

The Soviet Union is unlikely to show much interest in MBFR so long as the Politburo can anticipate unilateral Western reductions. And even if the Soviets should show an interest, a negotiated reduction would be long and difficult to achieve, because of the strategic asymmetries discussed in Chapter Six. Since the Warsaw Treaty Organization has no second-tier powers comparable to Britain, Germany, and France, the Soviet Union does not have in Eastern Europe what the United States has in Western Europe: allies with the human and material resources necessary for assuming a major share of the defense burden. On the other hand, the Soviet Union is not separated from its European allies by an ocean, and as a result the military consequences for it of withdrawing troops from Europe differ substantially from those for the United States.

The superpowers may discover that the troops most easily demobilized in Europe are those of their allies rather than their own. As was discussed in the preceding chapter, the Soviet Union needs to retain a superior military presence in Eastern Europe to deter political deviation or defection among its allies, and the United States has a political interest in maintaining an American presence large enough to prevent NATO from bearing a German military face. Similarly, if it is a question of withdrawing (but not demobilizing) troops presently stationed in Europe, the Soviet Union might find it difficult to move too many troops too far east without incurring charges of collusion from Peking. On its part, the United States, if NATO is to avoid an unbalanced look, might serve the cause of both MBFR and its balance of payments by having West German divisions moved to the United States for training, while trained American divisions remain in Germany.

VI

Formal negotiations with the Soviet Union on the range of issues extending from a NATO-WTO nonaggression pact to MBFR constitute, however, only one of the three major political arenas in which the United States can pursue its arms control objectives. A second and equally important arena is NATO itself. And for this arena an arms control issue of substantive importance is NATO policy for tactical nuclear weapons.

There would be need for Washington to engage its allies in a discussion of tactical nuclear-weapons policy in any event, but a review of present policy is especially in order, given the double prospect of unilateral reduction in American ground troops in Europe and strategic parity as a consequence of SALT. For in the wake of these developments the burden for both NATO's defense and NATO's deterrence increasingly would be placed on its tactical nuclear weapons.

The steeply rising curve of American tactical nuclear-weapons deployment in Europe over the past decade suggests the existence of few agreed-on criteria for determining the requirements for these weapons and further implies the absence of agreed-on criteria for their use. NATO currently has about 7000 nuclear warheads earmarked for tactical use—a force with more warheads and megatonnage than the United States will have in its submarine-launched missile force after the completion of the MIRV-Poseidon program. Obviously, if the NATO powers were actually to use all of these weapons in their defense and the Soviet Union were to reply in kind, Europe would be devastated. The interest of the Western Europeans is in deterrence, not in defense, and the role of tactical nuclear weapons is to confront the Soviet Union with the prospect that any attack on Western Europe would quickly escalate to a strategic exchange between the United States and the Soviet Union and thus deter a Soviet attack.

But it is by no means clear whether NATO's deployment, targeting doctrine, and command and control arrangements for tactical nuclear weapons are fully consistent with this purpose or indeed any other. The destruction that would attend the widespread use of tactical nuclear weapons coupled with a deployment of tactical air forces that makes them highly vulnerable to a first strike could, for example, provide both NATO and WTO with a strong incentive upon any outbreak of hostilities to undertake a massive preemptive use of tactical nuclear weapons.

How vulnerable are NATO's tactical nuclear forces to a first strike, and how great is the incentive for these forces to strike first? Does NATO doctrine anticipate a sparse, limited, and controlled use of tactical nuclear weapons, or are a large and wide variety of targets earmarked for quick destruction? What exactly are the command and control arrangements? Does the President release all at once the nuclear weapons earmarked for an individual NATO ally, and if so, who then decides on the use of such weapons? And by whom and how is the release of American-delivered weapons controlled? The very secrecy that surrounds these matters stimulates the hypothesis that if the information were available, the policies and postures concerned would prove to be uncertain, inconsistent, and uncoordinated.

The analysis previously advanced regarding the need for a war-ending as compared to a war-winning strategy, if deterrence should "fail," is as relevant for the use of tactical nuclear weapons as it is for strategic nuclear weapons. An agreement in principle on this matter would probably not be too difficult for NATO to reach. In the event of an outbreak of hostilities the Western Europeans have no greater interest in moving quickly to the massive use of tactical nuclear weapons than has the United States in moving quickly to an all-out use of strategic nuclear weapons. But if a common policy is reached on this issue, it will come as a result of political rather than military analysis and agreement. For at the heart of the problem is the question of whether NATO should gear its plans and preparations to the possibility of a deliberate Soviet assault on Western Europe or whether these plans and preparations should be made in the expectation that the more likely cause for the use of force in Western Europe will be a miscalculation on the part of one or both sides regarding the other's commitment to some part of the status quo.

The United States and its allies may meet with considerable difficulty, however, when they try to move from an agreement in principle to decisions in detail on the kind of deployment, doctrine, and command and control that would be appropriate to the use of tactical nuclear weapons in a war-delaying instead of a war-fighting capability and a war-ending instead of a war-winning strategy. There may be no way that NATO can avoid a stark choice between a strategy that increases time and choice (but also permits greater destruction in Western Europe if the Soviet Union does not practice similar restraint) and a strategy that could significantly reduce the initial damage that Western Europe might suffer after an outbreak of hostilities (but also lessens the opportunities for terminating the hostilities). This would be a consequential choice for NATO, and it will not be easily made, but the issues involved constitute one of the most significant arms control problems that the United States and its allies will face in the next decade.

VII

The third political arena in which Americans must pursue their arms control objectives is of course Washington itself, and it is here that Americans will confront the most immediate arms control issue of the decade: the future size of American conventional forces in Europe.

This chapter has stressed the critical importance of American troops in Europe for the stability of present European security arrangements: their key role in providing credibility for American strategic nuclear deterrence, their vital contribution to NATO's political deterrence against Soviet probes, and their clear advantage over tactical nuclear forces in a war-delaying strategy.

Unfortunately for arms control policy, the high priorities accorded domestic problems on both sides of the Atlantic, both sides of the English Channel, and both sides of the forty-ninth parallel have led to self-serving analyses of what each government regards as its fair and appropriate contribution to the common defense. There is a certain irony in the way many Europeans imply that Soviet power is so great that they must repeatedly question the credibility of the American nuclear guarantee and at the same time assert that the Soviet threat has so declined that it is safe to reduce their own country's level of sacrifice for national and NATO security. There is equal irony in the possibility that American exasperation with the "fair shares" problem may itself help move Western Europe toward free-ride, Sheltered Western Europe. And there is final irony in the possibility that public pressure in the NATO countries for troop reductions in Europe may have had the self-defeating effect of forestalling any immediate Soviet interest in negotiations toward that end.

On the major question that Washington must confront—how large an American military presence is required to demonstrate that the United States continues to have a vital interest in the security of Western Europe—no certain answer is possible. There is obviously no one and only number of divisions that can demonstrate this interest, but it is also obvious that however arbitrarily and accidentally determined is the present number of those divisions, a decrease will be an omen carefully read by friend and foe alike.

Four general guidelines for policy are apparent. First, if the United States is determined to reduce its forces in Europe, the new force level must not appear to the Western Europeans as either a *fait accompli* or a first step toward further reductions. If division and rancor among the NATO powers are to be minimized, the United States will need to consult with its allies in advance of any decision and to provide them with some assurance as to the stability of the decision once it is finally made.

Second, the greater the reduction in American troops, the greater its potential for altering political expectations. It may be unrealistic for Western Europeans and Russians to associate American policy in Europe with American policy in Vietnam and to equate a reduction in the American military presence in Western Europe with a reduction in the strength of the American political commitment, but it would also be unrealistic for Americans not to expect them to make this equation.

Third, there is no substitute for troops. Moscow might view increased American economic investment in Europe as a symbol of continued vital interest, but American leaders would be wise not to count on it; late twentieth-century Marxist-Leninists may not be so doctrinaire.

And fourth, troops in the United States are not the same as troops in Europe. Troops in Europe can help to deter crises; troops that return to Europe can at most help to resolve crises and may, in the act of returning, worsen them. Moreover, troops that can "come back" quickly to Europe can also "go forth" just as quickly somewhere else; and in the post-Vietnam political climate, sea- and airlift capabilities are not likely to fare too well in the battle of the budget.

In view of these guidelines and the prospect that the Western Europeans would make an American withdrawal an occasion for reducing their own contributions to the common defense, the pressure for reducing American troops in Europe seems most ill-advised. In the uncertain and somewhat arbitrary world of defense policy, it is perhaps not too strong to say that the dollars spent on American troops in Europe have probably been the most cost-effective part of the American defense budget. It would be both tragic and unwise if the backlash against a war for peripheral stakes in Asia and the mounting expenditures of a partly self-stimulated strategic arms race were permitted to lead to a sizable reduction in American troops in Western Europe. For Europe remains the most important part of the globe for both American and Soviet interests, and it contains the only tinder from which an all-out nuclear war might conceivably start. The United States has every interest in not blurring its commitment to the status quo by reducing its military presence there.

VIII

This book began by citing several dilemmas—most importantly a central strategic dilemma—that American policy-makers might encounter in an effort to work toward both strategic arms control and European security. It remains now to note how some of the conclusions of this book point the way around those dilemmas.

The central strategic dilemma disappears once it is appreciated that nulear superiority is not necessary to deter a Soviet attack on Western Europe. Provided the American political commitment to Western Europe remains clear and is supported by a large conventional military presence and a more politically appropriate doctrine for tactical nuclear weapons, a continued effort to maintain strategic superiority is better seen as a present luxury and a future invitation to danger than as an essential requirement for NATO security.

So far as European security is concerned, the United States is therefore free to enjoy both "savings now and safety later" through a strategic arms control agreement with the Soviet Union. Moreover, once the security of Western Europe is decoupled from American nuclear superiority, the apparent incompatibility between the need for alliance solidarity and progress toward a Soviet-American détente through arms limitations is also eased.

Other dilemmas appear less difficult once it is recognized that the security of Western Europe is provided with a substantial margin of deterrence that can be traded away for other valuable security objectives. At the margin consultation among allies may be more important than automaticity of nuclear-guarantee implementation, and forestalling miscalculation may be more important than a deterrent strategy that keeps the opponent guessing. Finally, since war by miscalculation is a greater danger and affords a greater opportunity for arms control than war by failure to deter, the apparent incompatibility between war-deterring and war-delaying strategies (which is the same as that between war-winning and war-terminating strategies) can be resolved in favor of delaying and ending.

As for the specific military policies best suited to serve the twin goals of strategic arms limitation and European security, the burden of this present chapter is that these goals will require a careful mix of arms, negotiated arms agreements, and arms self-control. Is this a mix that the United States government will be free to choose in the 1970s? The answer will be *no* unless Americans can develop among both officials and publics a more discriminating and conditional support for military policies than they have shown to date.

Military policy needs to be seen in broader terms than simply a choice between more or fewer arms or between increased or reduced military expenditures. Wise military policy requires a capacity for selective arms restraint as well as for selective arms maintenance. It is partly a matter of choosing not to have weapons and not to make defense expenditures that are redundant and wasteful at the moment and provocative in their effect on the opponent's own defense calculations. It is also a matter of choosing to have the weapons and make the sacrifices that demonstrate an American capability to support vital objectives and thus avoid luring an enemy into war by miscalculation. Finally, it is a matter of choosing to accept in international agreement those arms limitations and controls that the discovery of shared or compatible interests make possible and desirable.

Choices of this order are not easy to make; they will become impossible if the public and governmental debate on military policy continues to polarize between those who unconditionally favor more arms, no arms restraint, and few arms agreements and those who unconditionally favor fewer arms, unreciprocated restraints, and agreements for agreements' sake. Both elements of opinion will prove equally unhelpful to policy-makers charged with providing the greatest American security and the greatest assurance of world peace at the least material and human cost.

appendix: a note on
a methodology of projection

SCHOLARLY RESPONSIBILITY demands an explanation of how the pathways described in Chapter Five were constructed. First, as the reader will note in the explanations below, the analysis is not quantitative, but the thinking was. The authors conceptualized in terms of discrete variables ranged along defined continuums and projected partly on the basis of assumed bivariate relationships among the variables. Second, the analysis, although not theoretically sophisticated, is theoretically founded. Stability and change are treated as systemic outcomes produced through interaction sequences implicit in a simple systems model. The projections follow from a simplified systems analysis.[1]

Equilibrium in the European Security System

Looking into the plausible European future required defining the present in systems analysis terms. Accordingly, the European security system *circa* 1969 was defined as a reasonably stable multivariate equilibrium among twelve variables. The variables are

[1] In some of its aspects the model resembles Richard Rosecrance's abstractions from the international system; see his *Action and Reaction in World Politics* (Boston: Little, Brown and Company, 1963), pp. 220–32. The implicit dynamics of the model, however, follow more closely from Karl W. Deutsch's applied cybernetics; see his *The Nerves of Government* (New York: The Free Press, 1963), pp. 75–97. Techniques of systems analysis are distinguished by

listed in Appendix Table 1 along with their respective ranges of variation.

Chapters One through Four of this book indicate why the twelve variables in Table 1 were selected as components of a model European security system. The aim was to include all factors and forces that were deemed by the project staff and other knowledgeable analysts and observers to be essential in the equation of European security during the 1970s. It should be pointed out that for operational purposes each variable can and should be disaggregated into subvariables. Western European Capability for Self-Defense, for example, includes such subfactors as Western European Capability for Further Political and Military Integration, Western European Willingness to Integrate Further, and Western European Resources Available for Building an Autonomous Defense.

Appendix Table 2 parsimoniously describes what the European security system "looked like" in 1969 (or at least what the authors thought it looked like). The twelve variables were assumed to be in equilibrium at values given in the table. The equilibrium, moreover, was assumed to be rather stable, because the values of the variables had not changed greatly in several years.[2]

From the Present Into the Future

After establishing the multivariate structure of equilibrium in the European security system of 1969, which amounts essentially to an

---

Charles McClelland in *Theory and the International System* (New York: Macmillan Company, 1966), pp. 90–113, and these are elaborated in great detail in E. S. Quade and W. I. Boucher (eds.), *Systems Analysis and Policy Planning* (New York: American Elsevier Publishing Company, 1968), pp. 1–19, 30–53, and *passim*.

[2] It is obvious that the term "values" is being used in a very loose qualitative sense. The variables have not been quantified (although with some imagination and an extensive data-processing effort, they could be quantified). The only assumption made is that variables change states along the continuums identified in Table 1. With some apologies to colleagues who might demand more rigor, the authors have used intersubjective judgment as the technique for assigning values to variables in the 1969 equilibrium. The technique for estimating changes in values of variables as the system is pushed into the 1970s might best be labeled intersubjective speculation. For this method the authors do not blush intellectually, because the "futures" literature has not ex-

Appendix Table 1 Component Variables in the European Security System

Variable	Range of Variation
Credibility of the American Nuclear Commitment to Defend Western Europe	From Credibility unquestioned to Credibility denied
American Physical Involvement in European Conventional Defense	From Troop levels greatly increased to American forces withdrawn
Western European Perception of American Qualitative/Quantitative Nuclear Superiority over the Soviet Union	From Perception of unquestioned superiority to Perception of unquestioned inferiority
Western European Perception of Threat from the Soviet Union	From Perception of greatly heightened military threat to Perception of greatly reduced military threat
Western European Capability for Self-Defense	From Capability for going it alone to Complete dependence for defense
Western European Willingness to Allocate Resources to Defense	From Willingness to make great increases in outlays to defense sector to Unwillingness to allocate any resources to defense sector
Importance of Western Europe in American Definition of National Security	From Western Europe defined as part of national self to Western Europe defined as peripheral to American security
Western European Apprehensions about Germany	From Perception of heightened political-economic-military threat from Germany to No perception of German threat
Western European Propensity to Challenge or Otherwise Deviate from American Foreign Policies, Global and Regional	From Enhanced adherence to American leadership to Widespread deviation over broad policy ranges
Western European Influence in NATO's Strategic Decision-Making	From Equal European-American partnership in strategic decision-making to Greatly enhanced hierarchy in strategic decision-making
Soviet-American Political-Military Détente	From End of Cold War to Threshold of World War III
Soviet Control in Eastern Europe	From Enhanced hierarchy and more vigorously enforced orthodoxy to Autonomous Eastern European state system

Appendix Table 2 Equilibrium Values of Component Variables of the European Security System Circa 1969

Variable	*Value in 1969 System*
Credibility of the American Nuclear Commitment to Defend Western Europe	Commitment perceived as credible largely because of American reputation for promises kept
American Physical Involvement in European Conventional Defense	Substantial (225,000) troops in West Germany; a total strength of 310,000 men in American forces in Western Europe
Western European Perception of American Qualitative/Quantitative Nuclear Superiority over the Soviet Union	United States perceived as superior in nuclear capability
Western European Perception of Threat from the Soviet Union	Perception of "Onslaught Westward" nominal; perception of possible crisis and escalation notable; overall perception of threat low, however
Western European Capability for Self-Defense	Low
Western European Willingness to Allocate Resources to Defense	Reluctance, mainly because of pressures for allocation to other sources
Importance of Western Europe in American Definition of National Security	Western Europe defined as part of national self
Western European Apprehensions about Germany	Latent, but definitely present
West European Propensity to Challenge or Otherwise Deviate From American Foreign Policies, Global and Regional	Political differences relatively frequent and manifest; differences of political-ideological principle rare
Western European Influence in NATO's Strategic Decision-Making	American dominance; marked Western European dissatisfaction
Soviet-American Political-Military Détente	Reduced tension; overtures to cooperation; little substance in détente
Soviet Control in Eastern Europe	Orthodoxy coercively enforced

elaboration of the Two Spheres Europe ideal type, the authors asked themselves, their colleagues, and experts and diplomats several questions: which among the twelve variables are likely to change in value over the next ten years, how and how much are their values likely to change, and what systemic adjustments would likely result from the changes? Thus the "raw data" base consisted initially of a collection of experts' judgments, impressions, and opinions.[3]

Two analytical instruments were then used to organize these data and to derive the patterns set forth in Chapter Five. First, tables were constructed, consisting of verbal descriptions that displayed patterns of bivariate relationship between pairs of the twelve variables.[4] The tables showed both the *direction* of relationship within variable dyads and the *elasticity* of relationship, i.e., the amount of change in one variable that could be expected from a given change in another. To repeat, the patterns of relationship were the results of the collective judgment of the authors and the

---

hibited a better method for moving into the political unknown and because the task here was not to predict, but to speculate about the range of the plausible.

[3] Systematic interviewing was conducted by Professors Kelleher and Puchala among the staffs of the Office of External Research of the Department of State and of Radio Free Europe. Professor Kelleher brought additional insights from informal interviewing in West Germany. Professor Marshall Shulman added notes on Soviet and Eastern European thinking and expectations. Dr. Wilfrid Kohl provided recent observations on French outlooks. Some Commonwealth colleagues, Alastair Buchan, Hedley Bull, and Laurence Martin, exposed themselves to probings. The combined project staff interviewed a large proportion of the Western European statesmen and scholars who visisted New York between 1968 and 1970. Research assistants scoured the "European futures" literature. Thus in lieu of tapping the attitudes and expectations of actual European and American political actors for the 1970s—a task that was infeasible in terms of resources and impossible because Soviet and Eastern European views were unobtainable—the staff focused upon the judgments of highly knowledgeable observers.

For contrast, the reader is invited to compare these methods with those of Karl W. Deutsch et al., *France, Germany and the Western Alliance* (New York: Charles Scribner's Sons, 1967); and Daniel Lerner and Morton Gordon, *Euratlantica: Changing Perspectives of European Elites* (Cambridge: M.I.T. Press, 1969).

[4] Since several pairs of variables were unrelated, twenty-eight bivariate relationships were actually considered.

observers and analysts consulted. Because no "hard" longitudinal data on the dyadic relationships were at hand, one could only speculate about these relationships in the future. Therefore, the analysis is only as sound as the assumptions are valid. It is notable, however, that very few of the assumed dyadic relationships were elastic. Most frequently a large change in an independent variable was required for even a small change in a dependent one. This would suggest, not surprisingly, that the Two Spheres Europe equilibrium is a highly stable one. But notable also is the fact that none of the assumed dyadic relationships was linear. Envisaged slopes steepened and thus elasticities increased at the extreme ends of most variable continuums, suggesting that a dramatic change in any one of the twelve component variables could substantially disturb the Two Spheres Europe equilibrium. Equipped with tables of dyadic relationships, the authors could discover what would automatically happen to the Two Spheres Europe equilibrium if the values of different variables changed minimally, moderately, or maximally.

The second analytical tool was introduced in deference to international political reality. Very little in international politics happens *automatically*. Thus the authors devised an international interaction process model that permitted the identification of points within interaction sequences at which governments could exercise choice. The model also permitted varying outcomes that depend upon varying options chosen by governments and upon the varying effectiveness of governments' actions. Appendix Chart 1 displays the process model.

In brief, action begins in the phase labeled "disturbance." Here the value(s) of one or more of the twelve component variables is (are) changed at the initiative of one or more of the actors in the European security system (i.e., the United States government, the Soviet government, Western European or Eastern European governments). "Disturbance" has no normative connotation. It refers simply to an initiating move that *disturbs* the Two Spheres Europe equilibrium.

If the disturbance, either in itself or by virtue of the fact that changes in the value of one variable produce changes in the values of others, results in or appears to be resulting in a status quo minus

Appendix Chart 1. Systematic Stability and Transformation

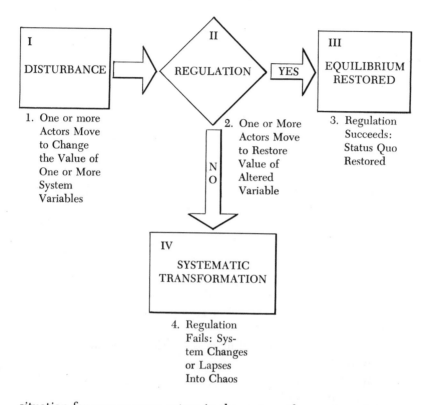

situation for one or more actors in the system, these actors, it is assumed, will react to the disturbance by making efforts to restore
the Two Spheres Europe equilibrium, as shown in the second
phase, "regulation." The regulation phase represents a "choice
point" for actors, and regulatory choice here consists of actors act-
ing to restore equilibrium by changing values of variables under
their control. For example, if the system is disturbed by Soviet actions which heighten Western European Perceptions of Threat, the
United States may attempt regulation by means of its control over
the Physical Involvement variable, its control over the NATO Decision-making variable or its partial control over the Superiority
variable. Similarly, Western Europeans may attempt regulation by
means of their control over the Willingness to Allocate Resources

to Defense variable, the Propensity to Deviate from American Positions variable or others.

Different choices among regulatory options as well as differential success at regulation can produce a variety of possible outcomes from any given disturbance. Thus much of the qualified, conditional, and admittedly circuitous wording in Chapter Five results from attempts to trace alternative outcomes from various postulated choices at regulatory choice points. Generally, however, outcomes are of two varieties—those that restore Two Spheres Europe equilibrium (bounce-back outcomes) and those that result in systemic transformation (i.e., from Two Spheres Europe to another security system).

Although the process model is very simple, it served its purpose well by injecting human voluntarism into the projections. It repeatedly forced the authors to ask and try to answer "Who can do and will do what, how, when, and why in response to different possible disturbances?"

The patterns of movement elaborated in Chapter Five evolved from the assumption, again based upon collective judgment, that five disturbances of the Two Spheres Europe equilibrium are plausible enough to be considered, namely:

1. Western European Willingness to Allocate Resources to Defense could deteriorate.

2. The Credibility of the American Nuclear Commitment to Western Europe could deteriorate.

3. Western European Material and Organizational Capacity for Self-Defense could increase.

4. Soviet-American Relations could improve or deteriorate dramatically.

5. Soviet Control in Eastern Europe could deteriorate.

Chapter Five is the result of attempts to assess the impacts of these disturbances by tracing relationships among component variables (e.g., if Western European Willingness to Allocate Resources to Defense deteriorates, what else is likely to change and how?) and then to follow disturbances from initiation to outcome along paths indicated by actors' options at regulatory choice points.

index